# The Measure of Poe

## BY LOUIS BROUSSARD

UNIVERSITY OF OKLAHOMA PRESS : NORMAN

By Louis Broussard

*American Drama: Contemporary Allegory from Eugene O'Neill to Tennessee Williams* (Norman, 1962)
*The Measure of Poe* (Norman, 1969)

Standard Book Number 8061-0859-2

Library of Congress Catalog Card Number: 69–16715

# Preface

THE IDEA THAT GOD IS DEAD is not new to the student of American literature. The religion of nature professed by Emerson, Thoreau, and Whitman, along with the skepticism recorded by Hawthorne, Melville, Dickinson, and Twain toward religious traditions, defines in good part the literature of the nineteenth century in America. What is not generally observed is that Emerson's rejection of a personal image for God found a disciple in Edgar Allan Poe and that Poe's own rejection of religious tradition found expression not only in the still unfamiliar prose-poem, *Eureka*, but in all his work as well, in the popular and well-known poems and short stories and in his criticism also.

The first part of this book offers a review of Poe criticism from 1845 to the present time. The second part offers an interpretation of Poe's poetry and fiction according to the principles he summarized in *Eureka*, and thus assigns Poe a unity of theme not acknowledged by a majority of his critics.

That the scientific principles Poe devised in *Eureka* are basic to an understanding of Poe's work is a theory which Margaret Alterton pioneered as long ago as 1925 in her "Origins of Poe's Critical Theory." Floyd Stovall wrote in 1931 that Poe is a poet of ideas and the ideas are there for those who will take the trouble to seek them out. The second part of this book proposes a more complete survey of Poe's work as a reflection of the conclusive *Eureka* than Miss Alterton and Hardin Craig offered in *Representative Selections* (1935) and emphasizes the change which Poe experienced in his view of life as death. Whereas the prevailing theme in the earlier work of Poe was life destined for a final disappearance, in *Eureka* death became the necessary dissolution in order that a reunion with Unity might occur. Near the end of his life Poe found the solution for the problem which had long plagued him. Life as a series of sorrows and disappointments became the process of gravitational and repulsive forces before the return to Unity.

This book attempts to assign a renewed emphasis, more complete than previously, to Poe's work as allegory and symbolism. As Professor Stovall has already pointed out, Poe's rejection of allegory and truth was the result of a desire to check the didactic tendencies among his contemporaries. Within the complete context of his meaning, Poe's stories and poems appear as allegorical illustrations of his truths, often projected through symbols which are not so effective as those of Yeats and Eliot, certainly, but which made way for them even before the symbolists. Poe established the foundations for twentieth-century symbolism—the atmosphere of its content and a logic for its use and acceptance.

Some, like W. H. Auden, have suggested that Poe may have been ahead of his time with the scientific attitudes advanced in *Eureka*. To Poe they were no more scientific than they were poetic. Creative activity, he wrote, is the thought of God, and man's imagination, which produces artistic creation, is but an extension of the divine talent. To see all of Poe's works as expressions of ideas is to know them as more than mere jingles about lost Lenores and

## Preface

Annabels or stories of terror and horror for their own sake. If there has been so much disagreement regarding Poe's merits, it is because few have seen him as an artist of ideas. Huxley saw him as a bad technician and, consequently, gave the impression that Poe was a poor writer because he was bad, technically, as a poet. Eliot, who could not accept Poe's views, close though they were to his own, arrived at an attitude of vindication for Poe only at the end of long travels in literature and criticism. A few studies of single works by Poe have witnessed their relationship to *Eureka*, but full-length studies of Poe continue to treat *Eureka* as an epilogue and not as a summary of principles worthy of evolutionary examination.

Biographies of Poe continue to emphasize the chronological appearance of his works, with little attempt to see them as parts of a unified philosophy. College instructors by and large treat Poe as a writer for children. We do not consider Emerson and Thoreau great poets, because they lacked sufficient poetic talent, but we do consider them great writers, having excelled in another form. Poe may not have been so great a poet as he was a critic and not so great a critic as he was a writer of short stories. Like all writers of genius, he was a man of ideas which found their way into everything he wrote, and some of his productions are better than others. Poe must be considered first of all as a creator of an artistic thought, which, from a scientific point of view as well, becomes increasingly interesting today in view of cosmological explorations.

*New York City*
*June, 1969*

LOUIS BROUSSARD

# Acknowledgments

I WISH TO THANK Sophie Ehrlich and Richard Erickson of New York City for their help in preparing this manuscript for publication.

I wish to thank also the following writers and their publishers for permission to quote from their publications: Vladimir Astrov, "Dostoievsky on Edgar Allan Poe," *American Literature*, Vol. XIV, Duke University Press; T. S. Eliot, *To Criticize the Critic*, Farrar, Straus & Giroux, Inc., and *Notes Towards a Definition of Culture*, Harcourt, Brace & World, Inc.; Aldous Huxley, "Vulgarity in Literature," *Saturday Review*, Vol. VII; Lois and Francis Hyslop, *Baudelaire on Poe*, Bald Eagle Press Books; D. H. Lawrence, *Studies in Classic American Literature*, The Viking Press, Inc.; Joseph Wood Krutch, *Edgar Allan Poe: A Study in Genius*, Russell & Russell, Inc.; Vernon L. Parrington, *Main Currents in American Thought*, Harcourt, Brace & World, Inc.; Allen Tate, "The Angelic Imagination: Poe and the Power of Words," *Essays of Four Decades*, The Swallow Press; Paul Valery, *Variety: Second Series*, Harcourt, Brace & World, Inc.; Edmund Wilson, *A Literary Chronicle: 1920–1950*, Farrar, Straus & Giroux, Inc.; and Yvor Winters, "Maule's Curse: Seven Studies in the History of American Obscurantism," *In Defense of Reason*, The Swallow Press.

# Contents

## LE TOMBEAU D'EDGAR POE

Tel qu'en Lui-même enfin l'éternité le change,
Le Poète suscite avec un glaive nu
Son siècle épouvanté de n'avoir pas connu
Que la mort triomphait dans cette voix étrange!

Eux, comme un vil sursaut d'hydre oyant jadis l'ange
Donner un sens plus pur aux mots de la tribu
Proclamèrent très haut le sortilège bu
Dans le flot sans honneur de quelque noir mélange.

Du sol et de la nue hostiles, ô grief!
Si notre idée avec ne sculpte un bas-relief
Dont la tombe de Poe éblouissante s'orne

Calme bloc ici-bas chu d'un désastre obscur
Que ce granit du moins montre à jamais sa borne
Aux noirs vols du Blasphème epars dans le futur.

—Stéphane Mallarmé, *Poésies*, 1887

PART ONE

*The Critical Estimate of Poe*

# Introduction

LONG AFTER POE'S DEATH his reputation continued to suffer
from traditions initiated by Rufus Griswold, his first biographer and editor. Griswold misrepresented Poe's character,
made changes in Poe's letters, recorded biographical inaccuracies like his explusion from the University of Virginia
and his desertion from the army, and labeled his talent
"erratic." Thus began for many the interest in Poe the man,
greater than the interest in Poe the writer, as a selfish, difficult, impotent eccentric, a dope addict, and a drunk. This
biographical interest, which diverted attention from the
significance Poe's content might possess, reached its climax
in Marie Bonaparte's Freudian interpretation of his writings
in 1933, which declared that Poe's work was a re-creation
of his neuroses—that his neuroses, so to speak, dictated his
works.

But the disagreement in the estimate of Poe's status cannot be satisfied with so simple an explanation. Griswold
was without doubt a critical cutthroat, but more damaging
statements have been made of Poe's work than his, some of
them after Woodberry and Quinn had exposed Griswold's
falsifications. And even more important is that prominent
writers, in both the last century and this one, who could
not have been influenced by biographical tradition, have
expressed their dislike for Poe's work. Edmund Wilson's

3

observation is interesting but hardly conclusive: "It seems hard to explain the virulence with which Griswold pursued him after his death and the general hostility toward him which has haunted us ever since, except on the ground that he puts us out by making so much of our culture seem second-rate."[1] The fact of Poe's popularity despite critical disfavor was stated well by Horace Gregory: "It can be safely said that the works of Edgar Poe are better known than the poetry of Longfellow or of Whitman or the novels of Hawthorne, Melville, and Henry James. In contrast to this picture, only the critical attitude seems ill at ease."[2]

Freedom from biographical prejudice cannot alone determine complete objectivity, and the critics of Poe may be subject to their own preferences for form or content or even to their failure to witness Poe's work—the poems, the short stories, the criticism—as a unit of expression, all reflective of a common theme. Poe wrote a great deal in each of these areas. He virtually created the short story as a form and gave it the most imaginative and original setting and characters possible, and because his form and content subscribed so strictly to his own rules, his stories must either appeal to the reader a great deal or not at all. The very nature of Poe's work confines the range of its appeal. His criticism, too, is likewise restricted in its appeal, so specific did he make the rules for writing a story or a poem. When Henry James put forth his principles of total recall and accurate boundaries within which to confine the narrative, he presented, not rules for writing, but rather necessary realizations for a realistic re-creation. Poe, on the other hand, wrote a rule book which calls upon the writer to do this, do that, this

[1] "Poe as a Literary Critic."
[2] "Within the Private View: A Note to Re-reading the Poetry of Edgar Allan Poe."

first, this next, this last. His poems lack the excellence of his short fiction, certainly, and without the interest in the poems as expressions of the same philosophy which created the short stories and even the critical essays, the critic may conclude that Poe was a poor poet and therefore a bad writer. The critic especially sensitive to Poe's poetic form or to the unreal content of his fiction or to his presumptuous critical method may lean to the conclusion that Poe is not a genius at all but a fake, a conclusion dependent upon a phase of his work rather than upon his total expression. A spiritual thinker like T. S. Eliot may even be unconsciously influenced by what must seem to a traditionalist to be heretical proclamations in *Eureka*.

The failure of the critic to recognize in a writer's work a unity of expression, of content—a philosophy traceable in it all, provided, of course, that unity is there—can result only in a distorted view. But to see Poe's body of work as a philosophy of composition is, perhaps, to realize that Poe, like all writers, sometimes excelled in his expression of his meaning and at other times did not, excelling often enough, however, to establish a literature of artistic merit.

# The Critical Estimate of Poe
# in the Nineteenth Century

JAMES RUSSELL LOWELL was the first to take critical notice of Poe, in *Graham's Magazine*, February, 1845. Lowell wrote the essay, at Poe's request, for a series entitled "Our Contributors" in *Graham's*. In it, Lowell attributed to Poe "that indescribable something which men have agreed to call *genius*." As a critic Lowell hailed him as "the most discriminating, philosophical, and fearless critic upon imaginative works who has written in America." Perhaps the most interesting statements in the essay are those which praise both the imaginative content and the form of Poe's short stories.

In his tales Mr. Poe has chosen to exhibit his power chiefly in that dim region which stretches from the very utmost limits of the probable into the weird confines of superstition and unreality. He combines in a very remarkable manner two faculties which are seldom found united: a power of influencing the mind of the reader by the impalpable shadows of mystery, and a minuteness of detail which does not leave a pin or a button unnoticed.
Beside the merit of conception, Mr. Poe's writings have also that of form. His style is highly finished, graceful, and truly classical. It would be hard to find a living author who had displayed such varied powers. As an example of his style we would refer to one of his tales, "The

7

House of Usher," in the first volume of his *Tales of the Grotesque and Arabesque*. It has a singular charm for us, and we think that no one could read it without being strongly moved by its serene and somber beauty. Had its author written nothing else it alone would have been enough to stamp him as a man of genius, and the master of a classic style.

Lowell praised "To Helen" as a remarkable effort for a youth of fourteen, though he printed the revised version of 1843 written when Poe was thirty-four. Regarding "The Haunted Palace," which also appears in full in the essay, Lowell asked, "Was ever the wreck and desolation of a noble mind so musically sung?" And for "Lenore," also quoted, he wrote, "How exquisite, too, is the rhythm!" Edmund Wilson has suggested that Poe himself may have added this exclamation since he had substituted "Lenore" for another poem quoted by Lowell. "It is not for us," Lowell concluded, "to assign his definite rank among contemporary authors, but we may be allowed to say that we know of *none* who has displayed more varied and striking abilities."[1]

Arthur Hobson Quinn has already observed the change in Lowell's estimate when Lowell's essay was reprinted in Volume I of Griswold's edition of Poe in 1850. Quinn believes the alterations were made by Griswold, because Griswold had requested changes from Lowell and Lowell's replies are lost. Lowell's estimate of Poe as "the most discriminating, philosophical, and fearless critic" of "varied and striking abilities" yielded to a verdict considerably different in the reprinted essay: "As a critic Mr. Poe was aesthetically deficient. Unerring in his analysis of dictions,

[1] *Graham's American Monthly Magazine*, Vol. XXVI (Feb., 1845), 49-53.

metres, and plots, he seemed wanting in the faculty of per-
ceiving the profounder ethics of art."[2] More than likely
Lowell himself made the change, for in 1848 he had published A *Fable for Critics*, containing his description of Poe
as "three-fifths of him genius and two-fifths sheer fudge."
If there is any need to look further into Lowell's reversal of
attitude, the evidence can be found perhaps in the irritation
which Lowell must have felt upon reading Poe's review of
A *Fable for Critics* in February, 1849.

> The *Fable* is essentially "loose"—ill-conceived and feebly
> executed, as well in detail as in general. Some good hints
> and some sparkling witticisms do not serve to compensate
> us for its rambling plot (if plot it can be called) and for
> the want of artistic finish so particularly noticeable
> throughout the work—especially in its versification. In
> Mr. Lowell's prose efforts we have before observed a cer-
> tain disjointedness, but never until now, in his verse, and
> we confess some surprise at his putting forth so unpol-
> ished a performance. . . .
> . . . By the publication of a book at once so ambitious
> and so feeble, so malevolent in design and so harmless in
> execution, a work so roughly and clumsily yet so weakly
> constructed, so very different in body and spirit from
> anything that he has written before, Mr. Lowell has com-
> mitted an irrevocable *faux pas* and lowered himself at
> least fifty percent in the literary public opinion.[3]

Poe's review must have antagonized Lowell, and it may
well have sparked the change which gave Griswold his most
valued support.

Between Lowell's first estimate of Poe in 1845 and Poe's

[2] Griswold (ed.), *Works* of Edgar Allan Poe, I, vii–xiii.
[3] *Southern Literary Messenger*, Vol. XV (March, 1849), 189–91.

death in late 1849, there appeared another enthusiastic evaluation of Poe's work, from P. Pendleton Cooke in the *Southern Literary Messenger* for January, 1848. Cooke's article, which he prefaced with the statement that it was "a sequel to Mr. Lowell's memoir," praised "The Raven" (not yet published at the time of Lowell's critique) as "a singularly beautiful poem" and "Ligeia" as "a wonderful story, written to show the triumph of the human will even over death. . . . Truthlike as nature itself, his strange fictions show constantly the presence of a singularly adventurous, very wild, and thoroughly poetic imagination." Cooke was the first to call to the reader's attention Elizabeth Barrett's statement on Poe, from a letter recently received, he said. Sarah Helen Whitman in her defense of Poe in 1860 would also rely for support on Mrs. Browning's reaction to "The Raven" and "Mr. Valdemar's Case."

This vivid writing—*this power which is felt*—has produced a sensation here in England. Some of my friends are taken by the fear of it, and some by the music. I hear of persons who are haunted by the "Nevermore," and an acquaintance of mine who has the misfortune of possessing a bust of Pallas, cannot bear to look at it in the twilight. Then there is a tale going the rounds of the newspapers, about mesmerism, which is throwing us all into "most admired disorder"—dreadful doubts as to whether it can be true, as the children say of ghost stories. The certain thing in the tale in question is the power of the writer, and the faculty he has of making horrible improbabilities seem near and familiar.[4]

But it was with less enthusiasm that Elizabeth Barrett wrote about Poe to Robert Browning on January 26, 1846: "There

[4] *Southern Literary Messenger*, Vol. XIV (Jan., 1848), 34–38.

is poetry in the man, though, now and then, seen between the great gaps of bathos. . . . *Politian* will make you laugh— as "The Raven" made me laugh. . . . Some of the other lyrics have power of a less questionable sort."[5]

Two years after Cooke's laudatory statement in the *Southern Literary Messenger*, Poe died, and Griswold's obituary initiated the controversy which has been Poe's legacy ever since. Griswold's obituary, which he signed "Ludwig," appeared on October 9, 1849, in the New York *Tribune*. It began as follows:

> Edgar Allan Poe is dead. He died in Baltimore the day before yesterday. This announcement will startle many, but few will be grieved by it. The poet was known, personally or by reputation, in all this country; he had readers in England, and in several of the states of Continental Europe; but he had few or no friends; and the regrets for his death will be suggested principally by the consideration that in him literary art has lost one of its most brilliant but erratic stars.

To emphasize his estimate of Poe the man, Griswold quoted Bulwer's description of Francis Vivian in his novel, *The Caxtons*:

> There seemed to him no moral susceptibility; and, what was more remarkable in a proud nature, little or nothing of the true point of honor. He had, to a morbid excess, that desire to rise which is vulgarly called ambition, but no wish for the esteem or love of his species; only the hard wish to succeed—not shine, not serve—succeed, that he might have the right to despise a world which galled his self-conceit.

[5] *Letters of Robert Browning and Elizabeth Barrett Browning, 1845–1846* (New York and London, 1899), I, 429.

Quinn pointed out in his biography of Poe that Griswold omitted the quotation marks when he expanded the article into the "Memoir" for his edition of Poe, thereby permitting these lines to stand as his own characterization. The "Memoir" elaborated Griswold's charges against Poe as a writer, asserting that "some of his plagiarisms are scarcely paralleled for their audacity in all literary history" and concluding there could be "scarcely any virtue in either his life or his writings."[6]

As influential as Griswold's statement was in the decade to follow, kinder words for Poe were forthcoming. Only a month after Griswold reared his ugly head, in November, 1849, the *Southern Literary Messenger* published an appreciative article by John R. Thompson, who quoted from a recent letter received from Longfellow, who had not always been treated kindly by Poe in his reviews. Longfellow's tribute is touching.

"What a melancholy death," says Mr. Longfellow, "is that of Mr. Poe—a man so richly endowed with genius! I never knew him personally, but have always entertained a high appreciation of his powers as a prose-writer and a poet. His verse has a particular charm of melody, an atmosphere of true poetry about it, which is very winning. The harshness of his criticisms, I have never attributed to anything but the irritation of a sensitive nature, chafed by some indefinite sense of wrong."[7]

To Poe himself Longfellow had written on May 19, 1841:

You are mistaken in supposing that you are not "favorably known to me." On the contrary, all that I have read

[6] Griswold (ed.), *Works* of Poe, III, v–xxxix.
[7] *Southern Literary Messenger*, Vol. XV (Nov., 1849), 694–97.

from your pen has inspired me with a high idea of your power; and I think you are destined to stand among the first romance-writers of the country, if such be your aim.[8]

Quite the most effective defense of Poe came from George Graham, the publisher of *Graham's*, which Poe had edited from 1841 to 1842. Graham expressed in the most dramatic terms his dismay over the appearance of Griswold's damaging "Memoir" in his edition of Poe. "I knew Mr. Poe well—far better than Mr. Griswold," Graham declared, "and . . . I pronounce this exceedingly ill-timed and unappreciative estimate of the character of our lost friend *unfair* and *untrue*. . . . So dark a picture has no resemblance to the living man." He called Griswold's "Memoir" a "fancy sketch of a perverted, jaundiced vision." It was an act of revenge, said Graham, for "some raps over the knuckles" which Poe had given Griswold for his anthology, *The Poets of America*. Poe had, "in the exercise of his functions as critic, put to death, summarily, the literary reputation of some of Mr. Griswold's best friends; and their ghosts cried in vain for him to avenge them." Griswold was not competent enough to measure Poe, who "eludes the rude grasp of a mind so warped and uncongenial as Mr. Griswold's."[9]

But Graham was not influential, and the emotional defense of Poe by Sarah Helen Whitman in her little book, *Edgar Poe and His Critics*, in 1860, was not either. The critical climate of Poe's estimate after his death remained for the most part adverse. In 1856, when Volume IV of Poe's *Works* edited by Griswold appeared, the highly regarded *North American Review* published a long review of

[8] *Letters of Henry Wadsworth Longfellow* (Cambridge, Mass., 1966), II, 302.

[9] "Editor's Table. The Late Edgar Allan Poe," *Graham's*, Vol. XXXVI (March, 1850), 224–26.

Poe's career as man and writer which accepted Griswold's untruths and presented a critical estimate no more favorable than that which accompanied the *Works*. Though the review began with some praise for "The Raven" and "Annabel Lee" as "exquisitely beautiful poems" and conceded "several of his prose tales fully equal in imaginative power," the reviewer extended his reservations into a long expression of censure not much different from Griswold's verdict. Regarding Poe's poetry as a whole, "his work appears a rich and elaborately finished piece of art, but it lacks the *vis vitae* which alone can make of words living things." Regarding his poetic principles, "we need only observe that his limitation of the proper themes and uses of poetry would exclude all the noblest productions of the best poets of all times and every tongue." Regarding his fiction, "let one never look into Poe's fictions for instruction in matters pertaining to the interior or higher life." Regarding his critical evaluations, "He was a master analyst, and could readily reduce a literary performance into its original elements; but he did not always discern its animating principle." In the very mood which infused Griswold's "Memoir," the *North American Review* concluded that Poe possessed

> ... to its fullest extent, and in its most virulent form, the *cant of genius*; we mean that disposition exhibited by many of the erratic stars of literature to claim exemption on account of their peculiarly fine temperament, from the ordinary rules of morality, ever begging the indulgence and tender judgment of their fellows on the very score of superiority. . . .
>
> ... most assuredly should we pray for some more potent chemistry to blot out from our brain-roll forever, beyond the power of future resurrection, the greater part of what

has been inscribed upon it by the ghastly and charnel-hued pen of Edgar Allan Poe. Rather than remember all, we would choose to forget all that he has ever written.[10]

But while the critical reaction to Poe in America was for the most part negative in the 1850's, following his death and the publication of his collected *Works*, Charles Baudelaire in France was busily engaged in his defense. Between 1848 and 1865 he translated and evaluated for a French audience the work of the man he considered more than anyone else *"mon semblable, mon frère."* In addition to his translations of the short stories, some of which appeared in magazines, beginning with "Mesmeric Revelation" in 1848, and which were collected in 1856, 1857, and 1865,[11] Baudelaire translated "The Raven" into prose in 1853, *Gordon Pym* in 1858, and *Eureka* in 1863. Baudelaire published his first long study, "Edgar Poe, His Life and Works," in two installments in the *Revue de Paris* in 1852, and followed this with an introduction, based on the first study, for the *Histoires Extraordinaires* in 1856. For the second volume of translations, *Nouvelles Histoires Extraordinaires*, Baudelaire wrote a third essay, "New Notes on Edgar Poe." For magazine publication of the short stories, Baudelaire sometimes wrote enthusiastic prefaces.

America and Poe were not compatible, wrote Baudelaire.

. . . for Poe the United States was a vast cage, great counting-house, and . . . throughout his life he made grim efforts to escape the influence of that antipathetic environment. . . .

[10] *North American Review*, Vol. LXXXIII (Oct., 1856), 427–55.
[11] *Histoires Extraordinaires*, 1856; *Nouvelles Histoires Extraordinaires*, 1857; *Histoires Grotesques et Sérieuses*, 1865.

. . . Americans are practical people, proud of their industrial strength, and a little jealous of the old world. They do not have time to feel sorry for a poet who could be driven insane by grief and loneliness. . . . They are in such a hurry to succeed. Time and money are all that count. . . .

. . . his inner, spiritual life, as a poet or even as a drunkard, was nothing but a perpetual effort to escape the influence of this unfriendly atmosphere.[12]

Baudelaire defended Poe's choice of subject matter, his doctrine of beauty, and his exclusion of long poems and poetry that is utilitarian or moralistic. In a statement as true of his own verses as it is of Poe's, Baudelaire wrote in "New Notes on Poe" that pure poetry "does not have Truth as an object; it has only Itself."[13]

Baudelaire expressed his admiration for Poe most conclusively as early as 1852, in his preface for the publication of "Berenice" in *l'Illustration*.

Edgar Poe is not exclusively a poet and a storyteller; he is poet, storyteller, and philosopher. He is at the same time both a visionary and a scholar. That he produced a few bad and hastily composed works is not at all surprising; that is explained by his terrible life. But what will always make him worthy of praise is his preoccupation with all the truly important subjects, and those which are *alone* worthy of the attention of a *spiritual* man: probabilities, mental illnesses, scientific hypotheses, hopes and considerations about a future life, analysis of the eccentrics and pariahs of this world, directly symbolic buffooneries. Add to this ceaseless and active ambition

[12] *Baudelaire on Poe*, Critical Papers trans. and ed. by Lois and Francis Hyslop, Jr. (State College, Pa., 1952), 39, 40, 91.
[13] *Ibid.*, 139.

of his thought an exceptional erudition, an astonishing impartiality which is antithetical to his subjective nature, an extraordinary power of analysis and deduction, and the customary tautness of his writing,—and it will not seem surprising that we have called him the *outstanding* figure of his country.[14]

In an interesting but not very well-known—and probably not influential—statement, none other than Dostoievsky expressed his appreciation of the American writer. In 1861 the magazine *Uremia* published translations of "The Tell-Tale Heart," "The Black Cat," and "Devil in the Belfry," for which Dostoievsky wrote a preface. "What a strange, though enormously talented writer, that Edgar Poe!" declared the Russian writer, and he went on to praise the imaginative quality of Poe's work.

Moreover, there exists one characteristic that is singularly peculiar to Poe and which distinguishes him from every other writer, and that is the vigor of his imagination. Not that his fancy exceeds that of all other poets, but his imagination is endowed with a quality which in such magnitude we have not met anywhere else, namely the power of details.... Yet Edgar Poe presents the whole fancied picture or event in all its details with such stupendous plasticity that you cannot but believe in the reality of possibility of a fact which actually never has occurred and even never could happen.[15]

But if eminent writers like Baudelaire and Dostoievsky on the Continent were Poe's champions, American writers certainly were not. In his first collection of critical essays,

[14] *Ibid.*, 151–52.
[15] Vladimir Astrov, "Dostoievsky on Edgar Allan Poe," *American Literature*, Vol. XIV (1942), 70–74.

*French Poets and Novelists,* published in England in 1878, Henry James called Baudelaire "the victim of a grotesque illusion" who "went in search of corruption," and said the "reader . . . finds the beauty perverted by the ugliness" in Baudelaire. What the reader observes in Baudelaire's poetry, said James, is "a gentleman in a painful-looking posture, staring very hard at a mass of things from which, more intelligently, we avert our heads." The French poet compromised himself further, added James, by identifying himself with Poe.

> For American readers, furthermore, Baudelaire is compromised by his having made himself the apostle of our own Edgar Poe. He translated, very carefully and exactly all of Poe's prose writings, and, we believe, some of his very superficial verses. With all due respect to the very original genius of the author of the *Tales of Mystery*, it seems to us that to take him with more than a certain degree of seriousness is to lack seriousness one's self. An enthusiasm for Poe is the mark of a decidedly primitive state of reflection. Baudelaire thought him a profound philosopher, the neglect of whose golden utterances stamped his native land with infamy. Nevertheless, Poe was much the greater charlatan of the two, as well as the greater genius.[16]

Henry James did not consider Poe important enough to assign him an essay, but in his reviews of other authors he expressed the disfavor with which he looked upon Poe's work. Careful always to refer to Poe's "genius," unable to ignore the impression which Poe's work made even upon him, James managed to convey, nevertheless, that indica-

[16] "Baudelaire," in *French Poets and Novelists* (London, 1878); reprinted with introduction by Leon Edel (New York, 1964).

tions of worth in Poe are the exception. James's estimate of Poe the critic appears in the third part ("Early Writings") of *Hawthorne*.

There was but little literary criticism in the United States at the time Hawthorne's earlier works were published; but among the reviewers Edgar Poe perhaps held the scales the highest. He at any rate rattled them loudest, and pretended, more than anyone else, to conduct the weighing process on scientific principles. Very remarkable was this process of Edgar Poe's, and very extraordinary were his principles; but he had the advantage of being a man of genius, and his intelligence was frequently great. His collection of critical sketches of the American writers flourishing in what M. Taine would call his *milieu* and *moment* is very curious and interesting reading, and it has one quality which ought to keep it from ever being completely forgotten. It's probably the most complete and exquisite specimen of *provincialism* ever prepared for the edification of men. Poe's judgments are pretentious, spiteful, vulgar; but they contain a great deal of sense and discrimination as well, and here and there, sometimes at frequent intervals, we find a phrase of happy insight imbedded in a patch of the most fatuous pedantry.[17]

Walt Whitman, who was the only American writer to attend the ceremony when a memorial was placed above Poe's grave in Baltimore, on November 17, 1875, expressed in 1880 the very attitude toward Poe's poetry one would expect from a nature so different from Poe's. It was a sentiment to be echoed in the twentieth century by Ernest Hemingway.

[17] *Hawthorne* (London, 1879; New York, 1880), 62.

## The Measure of Poe

By common consent there is nothing better for man or woman than a perfect and noble life, morally without flaw, happily balanced in activity, physically sound and pure, giving its due proportion, and no more, to the sympathetic, the human emotional element—a life, in all these, unhasting, unresting, untiring to the end. And yet there is another shape of personality dearer far to the artist-sense, (which like the play of strongest lights and shades) where the perfect character, the good, the heroic, although never attained, is never lost sight of, but through failures, sorrows, temporary downfalls, is return'd to again and again, and while often violated, is passionately adhered to as long as mind, muscles, voice, obey the power we call volition. This sort of personality we see more or less in Burns, Byron, Schiller, and George Sand. But we do not see it in Edgar Poe. . . .

. . . Poe's verses illustrate an intense faculty for technical and abstract beauty, with the rhyming art to excess, an incorrigible propensity toward nocturnal themes, a demoniac undertone behind every page—and, by final judgment, probably belong among the electric lights of imaginative literature, brilliant and dazzling, but with no heat.

Whitman admitted that his distaste for Poe had at long last yielded to an acceptance of Poe's work for what it is, despite the "morbidity," the "abnormal beauty," the "sickliness." Like James, Whitman felt at odds with the temper of Poe's work but had to admit that "Poe's genius has yet conquered a special recognition for itself." Nevertheless, in a reference to the "lush and the weird that have taken such extraordinary possession of nineteenth century verse lovers," Whitman insisted that he still wanted for poetry "the clear sun shining, and fresh air blowing—the strength and power of health, not of delirium, even amid the stormiest passions—with always the background of the eternal moralities." Poe's spirit, his misadventures, his poems, were all "lurid dreams," said Whitman.[18]

The years between 1870 and 1880 were especially productive of biographical comment on Poe, most of it unfavorable. One article in *Scribner's* in 1875 attempted to prove Poe insane: "A Mad Man of Letters." After 1880 the attitude became more objective. Biographical studies by Stoddard, Ingram, and Woodberry attempted an unbiased view.[19] In 1889, Thomas Nelson Page pointed out that twenty-nine thousand copies of Poe's *Tales* had been sold in Britain in 1887 against one-third that number for other more famous American writers. In an article in *Lippincott's* in 1889, "Authorship in the South before the War," Page argued that "Poe's poetry discovered a fresh realism in the domain of fancy," that Poe's "critical faculty installed a new era in criticism," and that his "imaginative works created a new school." Page recorded in his estimate of Poe the critic what has come to be the consensus of opinion regarding Poe the critic in the second half of the twentieth century: "He lifted literary criticism from the abasement of a snivelling imbecility into which it had sunk, and established it upon a basis founded on the principles of analysis, philosophy, and art."[20]

In England an attitude contrary to America's rejection of Poe had for some time existed. In 1872, Swinburne had

18 "Edgar Poe's Significance," in *Specimen Days, Complete Prose of Walt Whitman*, I, 284–87.

19 John H. Ingram, *Edgar Allan Poe; His Life, Letters, and Opinions* (London, 1880); George Woodberry, *Edgar Allan Poe* (Boston, 1885); R. H. Stoddard included a biographical introduction in his edition of Poe in six volumes in 1884.

20 *Lippincott's Monthly Magazine*, Vol. XLIV (July, 1889), 105–20.

written his appreciation of Poe's "exquisite music."[21] In 1893, Edmund Gosse, in an essay entitled "Has America Produced a Poet?" regretted that "Edgar Allan Poe is still unforgiven in New England," and while he made allowances for Poe's weaknesses and shortcomings, Gosse felt "the perennial charm of his verses." His statement accounting for Poe's failure to rank with the greatest may well be the best explanation yet for the lingering Poe controversy.

> If the range of the Baltimore poet had been wider, if Poe had not harped so persistently on his one theme of remorseful passion for the irrevocable dead, if he had employed his extraordinary, his unparalleled gifts of melodious invention, with equal skill, in illustrating a variety of human themes, he must have been with the greatest poets.

Gosse concluded that Poe's technical artistry, though narrow in its range of expression, and his influence on the succeeding generation of artists were enough "to have deserved great honour from the country of his birthright."[22]

John Burroughs took issue with Gosse in the same year in an article entitled "Mr. Gosse's Puzzle over Poe."

> Poe, like Swinburne, was a verbal poet merely; empty of thought, empty of sympathy, empty of love for any real thing. . . . I would not undervalue Poe. He was a unique genius. But I would account for his failure to deeply impress his own countrymen, outside the professional literary guild. His fund of love and sympathy was small. He was not broadly related to his fellows, as were Longfellow and Whittier and Whitman. His literary

[21] *Under the Microscope* (London, 1872), 53.
[22] *Questions at Issue* (London, 1893), 188–90.

equipment was remarkable; his human equipment was not remarkable: hence his failure to reach the general fame of the New England poets.[23]

It was a chance remark made by Emerson ten years after Poe's death and recorded by Howells just before the close of the century which proved to be the most influential commentary of all. In 1900, William Dean Howells published *Literary Friends and Acquaintances* and in the chapter entitled "My First Visit to New England" told of his visit with Emerson in Concord forty years earlier, when Emerson was sixty and Howells only twenty-three.

> After dinner we walked about in his "pleached garden" a little, and then we came again into his library, where I meant to linger only till I could fitly get away. He questioned me about what I had seen of Concord, and whom besides Hawthorne I had met, and when I told him only Thoreau, he asked me if I knew the poems of Mr. William Henry [Ellery?] Channing. I have known them since, and felt their quality, which I have gladly owned a genuine and original poetry; but I answered then truly that I knew them only from Poe's criticisms: cruel and spiteful things which I should be ashamed of enjoying as I once did.
>
> "Whose criticisms?" asked Emerson.
>
> "Poe's," I said again.
>
> "Oh," he cried out, after a moment, as if he had returned from a far search for my meaning, "you mean the jingle-man!"[24]

Just as Griswold's "Memoir" found its way into every complete edition of Poe's *Works* for half a century after

23 *The Dial*, Vol. XV (1893), 208–16.
24 New York, 1901, pp. 63–65.

Poe's death, so would Emerson's remark, Poe the "jingle-man," find its repetition in every introduction to Poe in every anthology of American literature published thereafter. Poe had called Longfellow a plagiarist; he had laughed at Channing's verse and Margaret Fuller's prose, and in "A Chapter on Autography" had written that "Mr. Ralph Waldo Emerson belongs to a class of gentlemen with whom we have no patience whatever—the mystics for mysticism's sake. . . . His love of the obscure does not prevent him, nevertheless, from the composition of occasional poems in which beauty is apparent in flashes." When Poe invoked the wrath of New Englanders upon his head, he solicited as well their influence upon his critical reputation for generations to come.

The general attitude toward Poe, then, at the close of the nineteenth century in America was summarized by Howells when he reported Emerson's verdict uttered forty years earlier. Poe was a jingle-man! Griswold had fired the opening shot against Poe's reputation, and the animosity created by Poe's dismissal of so much American writing lingered to substantiate Griswold's judgment. Poe continued to have defenders, however. One was Brander Matthews, who accepted the flaws but found reason for praise.

That his scheme of poetry was highly artificial, that the themes of his poems were vague and insubstantial, and that his stanzas do not stimulate thought—these things may be admitted without disadvantage. What the reader does find in Poe's poetry is the succession of departed but imperishable beauty, and the lingering grace and fascination of haunting melancholy. His verses throb with an inexpressible magic and glow with intangible fantasy. His poems have no other purpose; they convey no moral; they echo no call to duty; they celebrate beauty only—

24

beauty immaterial and evanescent; they are their own excuse for being.[25]

Poe's Continental reputation was perhaps enough to make other writers jealous. Some have pointed out that society was against Poe because it considered his life disgraceful and because Poe was a southerner at a time when sectional differences magnified prejudice. True, but the prejudice against Poe was also an intellectual prejudice, and we have but to summon the statements of James and Whitman as evidence. Poe was not part of the American tradition, or so it seemed to many in the nineteenth century and as it still seems to many in our own time. Emerson's philosophy emerged from Unitarian thought, which had succeeded the Puritan. So was Hawthorne related, in scene and tradition, to Americana. Thoreau and Whitman and Twain and even Dickinson were all part of evolutionary American principles. Melville, who was forgotten at the end of the century, was also part of the American scene, and even James, misinterpreted by some even now as anti-American, wrote with one eye at least on America. When Poe created his House of Usher, he created a world of his own imagination, and the realists who followed the Civil War could not witness his work except as an extension of Gothic romance. There was nothing transcendental about Poe; his scenes and his people were not American or even real, and the public had Poe's own declaration that poetry and fiction should not concern themselves with truth. Poe made a great deal of trouble for himself with his ambiguous denials of "truth" as the property of art.

Many readers could not identify with Poe's creation because the context of their own attitudes toward art and life

[25] *An Introduction to the Study of American Literature*, 166.

did not permit it. Lacking a complete understanding of Poe's work, they could not view it as an expression which transcends the immediate characteristics of locale and personage to reveal a truth as transcendental as that of Emerson himself. To them Poe's art was art for art's sake only. But more than even Poe himself realized perhaps, his work is as meaningful in an American or worldly context as the literature of realism. Nineteenth-century readers did not know *Eureka*, or if they did, they gave no indication of their acquaintance, and certainly they failed to identify Poe's work as a detailed expression of principles as fully transcendental and reactionary as anything else which appeared in America in a century of "democratic" expression.

# The Critical Estimate Since 1900

IN A REVIEW ENTITLED "A Hundred Years of American Verse" in the *North American Review* for January, 1901, William Dean Howells noted that "nature-worship runs all through" our literature but that "supernature-worship" is alien to all but Poe. "Was he then," asked Howells, "our great original?" As if in answer to his own proposal, Howells wrote, "Yet it is perversely possible that his name will lead all the rest when our immortals are duly marshalled for the long descent of time."[1]

In 1902, J. A. Harrison of the University of Virginia edited the seventeen-volume Virginia edition of Poe's *Works*, including Harrison's two volumes of *Life* and *Letters*. To those at the University of Virginia in 1900, to celebrate the centenary of Poe's birth, William Butler Yeats wrote a letter in which he pronounced Poe "the greatest of American poets, and always and for all lands a great lyric poet."

The most ambitious evaluation of Poe in the first decade of the new century was a long article in *Scribner's Magazine* by W. C. Brownell for January, 1909. In an attitude similar to that taken by all the descendants of Griswold,

[1] Howells' review of Edmund Clarence Stedman (ed.), *An American Anthology, 1787–1899*, in *North American Review*, Vol. CLXXII (Jan., 1901), 148–60.

# The Measure of Poe

Brownell declared that Poe had come at the close of an epoch. "He did not introduce one." His poetry is "overvalued because it answers the technical test, because in short it sounds well." Poe's criticism reflects no "culture or philosophical depth," and his analyses of his own art "show conclusively that his art was an art of calculation and not the spontaneous expression of a weird and gruesome genius that it seems to so many upon whom it produces its carefully prepared effect." Poe achieved atmosphere but "an atmosphere which is less the envelope than the content of his work. . . . Nothing takes place in 'The Fall of the House of Usher' that is not trivial and inconclusive compared with its successful monotone, its atmosphere of lurid murk and disintegrating gloom." In the attitude adopted by the realists toward Poe, Brownell agreed that it is "idle to endeavor to make a great writer of Poe because . . . his writings lack the elements not only of great, but of real, literature." Poe's work is "not sensuous but scenic," and "so appalling an egoist" was lacking in humor and heart. "The cult of Poe," Brownell concluded, "is not in the interests of literature, since as literature his writings are essentially valueless."[2]

A great contribution to Poe scholarship was made in 1917. Killis Campbell edited *The Poems of Edgar Allan Poe* and included a long introduction containing a sympathetic life of the writer and commentaries on Poe's revisions, his indebtedness to other writers, and the estimates made of Poe since his death. Campbell's main source was the 1845 edition of thirty poems. He corrected the errors made by Griswold in his edition, and he included the textual variations introduced by subsequent editors as well. Poe's poetry had at long last come under close scrutiny, and the results were carefully and scholarly recorded.

[2] *Scribner's,* Vol. XL (Jan., 1909), 69–84; reprinted in *American Prose Masters.*

In the *English Review* in 1919 appeared D. H. Lawrence's study of Poe, which Lawrence would later include in *Studies in Classic American Literature* in 1923. Lawrence was the first to apply Freudian psychology to an understanding of Poe, who, he said, was "absolutely concerned with the disintegration-processes of his own psyche" and whose best pieces are "ghastly stories of the human soul in its disruptive throes."

Poe had a pretty bitter doom. Doomed to seethe down his soul in a great continuous convulsion of disintegration, and doomed to register the process. And then doomed to be abused for it, when he had performed some of the bitterest tasks of human experience, that can be asked of a man. Necessary tasks, too. For the human soul must suffer its own disintegration, *consciously*, if ever it is to survive.

He was an adventurer into vaults and cellars and horrible underground passages of the human soul. He sounded the horror and the warning of his own doom.

Doomed he was. He died wanting more love, and love killed him. A ghastly disease, love. Poe telling us of his disease: trying even to make his disease fair and attractive. Even succeeding.

Lawrence introduced a new variation to the biographical interest in Poe—the Freudian fate which would inevitably overtake all writers. Students of Poe's sex life would be legion thereafter, and foremost among them were Joseph Wood Krutch and Marie Bonaparte.

*Edgar Allan Poe, A Study in Genius* (1926) traces Poe's art, said its author, Joseph Wood Krutch, "to an abnormal condition of the nerves" and his critical principles " to a rationalized defense of the limitations of his own taste." The abnormal nerve condition was sexual impotence, the result of a mother fixation. Being unable to participate in the normal world of sex relations, Poe created his own domain of horror and destruction in which he found escape from his dilemma. Poe always felt the need to justify himself. He sought literary fame as a substitute for the social position he lost when his foster father rejected him. He created his own world of fiction as a substitute for the real world in which he could not function, and he justified his artistic methods with essays of critical theory. Of the many allusions to the relationship between Poe's art and his sex life, the account by Krutch is the most succinct.

> . . . if we compare the typical stories already described with the story of Poe's own life, it is impossible not to be struck with the parallel which they afford. The typical hero, oppressed with a strange melancholy and seeking relief in fantastic studies and speculations, is plainly Poe himself. The heroines with the unearthly beauty and the unhealthy purity which seem to set them apart from the women of flesh and blood are not exactly Virginia, but they are the phantoms to whom she, with her morbid fragility and child-like mind, seemed better to correspond than any other woman whom Poe had ever seen. And, most important of all, both she and they carried about them no suggestion of physical passion but could be loved by one to whom the whole idea of physical union was utterly repulsive. They are the ideal of morbidly sexless beauty.

Thus if we compare the most striking action of Poe's life with his most characteristic stories, the two seem to spring from the same impulse, the one representing his attempt to adjust himself to actuality and the other his attempt to create, after the manner of neurotics, an imaginary world to fit the needs of his mind. Of all the stories which deal with the relations between a man and a woman only two indicate even by implication the possibility of normal union, and in both the result of this union is wholly evil. Something unearthly in the woman seems to stand between her and the hero, and death soon comes to remove her, leaving him safe to dream over merely the idea of a woman instead of a woman herself.

The objection to the kind of book Krutch has written was voiced by Edmund Wilson in a piece called "Poe at Home and Abroad" in the *New Republic* of December 8, 1926. Such studies, said Wilson, supply an interpretation of the writer's personal career but neglect to explain why we should still want to read him. "In respect to such figures as Poe, we Americans are still perhaps almost as provincial as those of their contemporaries who now seem to us ridiculous for having failed to recognize their genius." Wilson accused Krutch of "misunderstanding Poe's writings and seriously undervaluing them" and even "caricaturing them —as the modern school of social-psychological biography, of which Mr. Krutch is a typical representative, seems inevitably to tend to caricature the personalities of its subjects; . . . he tells us, in effect, that Poe wrote like a dispossessed Southern gentleman and a man with a fixation on his mother."

Wilson argued that one must look for meaning in Poe on romantic terms. We should not expect from his work the same treatment of life that we find in Theodore Dreiser or Sinclair Lewis. As a typical romantic, Poe achieved in his verse "the indefiniteness of music—that supreme goal of the symbolists." Poe's short stories find their significance, not in what they relate, but in the effect which the dream-like narrative creates. Wilson appealed for support to Poe's own declaration that the "skillful artist" first conceives a "single effect" and then invents incidents to establish the preconceived effect.

No one understood better than Poe that, in fiction and in poetry both, it is not what you say that counts, but what you make the reader feel (he always italicizes the word "effect"); no one understood better than Poe that the deepest psychological truth may be rendered through phantasmagoria. Even the realistic stories of Poe are, in fact, only phantasmagoria of a more circumstantial kind.

Any realism of any age which does not convey some truth is, of course, bound to be unsatisfactory. And today when a revolt is in progress against the literalness and the superficiality of the naturalistic movement that has come between Poe's time and ours, he ought to be of special interest.[3]

The climax to the Freudian interest in Poe generated by Lawrence was Marie Bonaparte's *Edgar Poe: Etude Psychoanalytique* in 1933.[4] According to Miss Bonaparte, Poe's fiction and poetry are re-creations of emotional fixations which were the result of infantile experience. Though all his work is representative, "Ligeia" is her classic example. Rowena reincarnates both Mrs. Allan and Virginia, in whom Poe betrayed the mother, whose return signifies a reunion with the loved object in death, death already linked in the unconscious with the prenatal, fetal state. In spite of repeated efforts to flee, Poe was never able to free himself. The mother never relinquished her prey, and in other significant works like "Annabel Lee" and "Ulalume,"

---

[3] Wilson, "Poe at Home and Abroad"; reprinted in A *Literary Chronicle, 1920–1950.*

[4] Later to appear in English translation as *Life and Works of Edgar Allan Poe,* with foreword by Sigmund Freud.

Poe reiterated how, in his unconscious, he remained faithful to the mother.

For many a reviewer or critic in the twenties, Poe's work became reading matter for adolescents; his pseudo-Gothic re-creations were not compatible with the new investigations into reality being made by the Joyceans and the Fitzgeralds and the Hemingways. The literati, preoccupied with their interpretations of *Ulysses* and *The Waste Land*, inclined to a point of view expressed some years earlier by Brownell when he said, "Mainly, I imagine, Poe's stories are read in youth and rarely returned to." But they were always hounded by the influence which Poe seemed to exert on Continental writers who in time would drive home to the new realists and the new humanists the significance of Poe as, perhaps, the first symbolist in English and even the beginning of a tradition in poetry which reached its climax in "Prufrock."

In what was probably the grandest reassessment of American values yet attempted, Vernon Parrington in *Main Currents in American Thought* in 1927 assigned historical importance to Poe as an early romanticist but emphasized that whatever merits Poe's work might have, it had from the beginning been antagonistic to American ideals.

> His romanticisms were of quite another kind than those his countrymen were pursuing; and the planter sympathized with them no more than did the New York literati or the western men of letters. In a world given over to bumptious middle-class enthusiasms, there would be scant sympathy for the craftsman and dreamer. . . .And so, like Herman Melville, Poe came to shipwreck on the reef of American materialisms. The day of the artist had not dawned in America. . . .
>
> . . . Whatever may be the final verdict it is clear that

33

as an aesthete and a craftsman he made a stir in the world that has not lessened in the years since his death, but has steadily widened. . . . He was the first of our artists and the first of our critics; and the surprising thing is that such a man should have made his appearance in an America given over to hostile ideals. He suffered much from his aloofness, but he gained much also. In the midst of gross and tawdry romanticisms he refused to be swallowed up but went his own way, a rebel in the cause of beauty, discovering in consequence a finer romanticism than was before known in America.

Two years after *Ulysses* and *The Waste Land*, George Moore published his *Anthology of Pure Poetry*, which included six poems by Poe, a larger number than that of any other poet except Shakespeare.[5] But if George Moore, a lingering traditionalist, liked Poe's poems, which were to him, he said in his introduction, "almost free from thought," an Englishman from the brave new world did not. In 1930, Aldous Huxley expressed in *Vulgarity in Literature* his astonishment at the esteem in which the French poets held Poe, and he tried, before Eliot, to account for Baudelaire's enthusiasm for Poe's poetics.

> We who are speakers of English and not English scholars . . . we can only say with all due respect, that Baudelaire, Mallarmé, and Valéry are wrong and that Poe is not one of our major poets. . . . The substance of Poe is refined; it is his form that is vulgar. . . .
> . . . How could a judge so fastidious as Baudelaire listen to Poe's music and remain unaware of its vulgarity?

[5] New York, 1925. The six poems are: "To Helen," "The Valley of Unrest," "Dreamland," "The City in the Sea," "The Haunted Palace," and "Ulalume."

A happy ignorance of English versification preserved him, I fancy, from the realization.[6]

If Huxley hoped to dismiss Poe's poetry from the pages of literature, the French as usual were there to attend to the rescue. In the same year, 1930, Paul Valéry in his essay, "Situation de Baudelaire," in *Varieté*, repeated remarks he had made earlier in an introduction for an edition of *Les Fleurs du Mal* in 1926. He summarized Poe's contributions as follows:

> Thus it is not astonishing that Poe, possessing so effective and sure a method, should be the inventor of several varieties, should have offered the first and most striking example of the scientific tale, of the modern cosmogonic poem, of the novel of criminal investigation, of the introduction into literature of morbid psychological states, and that all his work should manifest on every page an intelligence which is to be observed to the same degree in no other literary career. This great man would today be completely forgotten had not Baudelaire introduced him into European literature. Let us not fail to observe here that Poe's universal glory is weak or contested only in his native country and England. This Anglo-Saxon poet is strangely neglected by his own race.

As if in direct reply to Huxley, Valéry explained Baudelaire's affinity for Poe as an identity of values.

> Baudelaire and Edgar Allan Poe exchanged values. Each gave to the other what he had, received from the other what he had not. The latter communicated to the former a whole system of new and profound thought. He

---

[6] Chapter 6; appeared as article in *Saturday Review*, Sept. 27, 1930.

enlightened him, he enriched him, he determined his opinions on a quantity of subjects: philosophy of composition, theory of the artificial, comprehension and condemnation of the modern, importance of the exceptional and of a certain strangeness, an aristocratic attitude, mysticism, a taste for elegance and precision, even politics. . . . Baudelaire was impregnated, inspired, deepened by them.[7]

Not too long after Huxley and Valéry, Ernest Hemingway pronounced his one-sentence dismissal of Poe in *Green Hills of Africa*: "Poe is a skillful writer. It is skillful, marvelously constructed, and it is dead." Hemingway's impression recalls Whitman's description of Poe's work: "brilliant and dazzling, but with no heat." "The good writers," said Hemingway, "are Henry James, Stephen Crane, and Mark Twain."[8]

Probably the most damning words spoken against Poe and the least objective were recorded by Yvor Winters in "Edgar Allan Poe: A Crisis in the History of American Obscurantism," which first appeared in *American Literature* in 1937 and was afterward reprinted in *Maule's Curse* in 1938. Winters called Poe "a bad writer . . . an excited sentimentalist . . . obscurantist . . . his crudity obvious."

He understood little or nothing that was written before his own age. . . . We can scarcely avoid the observation that his work is compounded almost wholly of stereotyped expressions, most of them of a very melodramatic cast.

To illustrate the weakness of detail in his poems and stories is no easy matter; to illustrate the extent of that

[7] Paul Valéry, *Variety: Second Series*, 71–98.
[8] New York, 1935, p. 20.

weakness is impossible, for his work is composed of it. . . . We are met on every page of his poetry with resounding puerilities such as "the pallid bust of Pallas," and "the viol, the violet, and the vine." . . . This is an art to delight the soul of a servant girl; it is a matter of astonishment that mature men can be found to take this kind of thing seriously.

It is unlikely . . . that the course of romantic literature would have been very different except (perhaps) in America, had Poe never been born; in any event, his influence could only have been a bad one, and to assert that he exerted an influence is not to praise him.

Winters' only concession was that Poe had been consistent in theory and practice, but he was quick to add that Poe had been "exceptionally bad in both." As for his being a mystic, Poe was "no more a mystic than a moralist."

Other academicians were more appreciative of Poe. Margaret Alterton, Hardin Craig, and Floyd Stovall interpreted the "idea" in Poe's work and made significant contributions toward the establishment of Poe as a writer of substance. Margaret Alterton's "Origins of Poe's Critical Theory" (1925) and the introduction and notes to *Representative Selections* (1935), begun by Miss Alterton and completed by Hardin Craig, are two of the most important critiques yet written about Poe.

The best biography of Poe, as well as the best exposition of the literary background of his time, is Arthur Hobson Quinn's *Edgar Allan Poe: A Critical Biography*, which appeared in 1941. Hervey Allen's *Israfel* in 1926 had re-examined Poe's relationship with John Allan, the letters between them having been published in 1925, but Quinn's contribution was far more significant. Quinn exposed Griswold as a forger and so put an end to that phase of the Poe controversy. Quinn revealed Griswold's forgeries, not only in the letters written by Poe but also in those written to him. Several biographies of Poe have appeared since Quinn's, but they are merely re-creations, shorter versions, and they do not add anything about Poe the man or the circumstances surrounding the composition of his work.[9]

In sharp contrast with Huxley and Winters, Horace Gregory, a poet himself before he took to criticism, concluded upon having re-read Poe in 1943 that despite its flaws Poe's work retains its appeal, for the common reader at least if not for the critic.

> His failures may be obvious enough, failures of taste, proportion and adult responsibility, but with the possible exception of his essay on "The Rationale of Verse," he is never dull—and it would be a rare phenomenon indeed to find a reader who had fallen asleep in the progress of following the plot of one of Poe's tales.[10]

Professional criticism after Winters was more objective and inclined to accept Poe's eminence in American letters. In 1945, Malcolm Cowley in the *New Republic* called his review of the Viking Portable edition of Poe, "Aidgarpo," and while he conceded that in Baudelaire's translation Poe "stands clear of the rubbish with which his grave has been encumbered," he accepted Poe as a worthy forerunner of many a contemporary tradition.

> He stands at the exact beginning of the doctrine of art

[9] Allen, *Israfel: The Life and Times of Edgar Allan Poe* (New York, 1926); Quinn, *Edgar Allan Poe: A Critical Biography* (New York, 1941); Mary Newton Stannard, *Letters Till Now Unpublished* (Philadelphia and London, 1925).

[10] "Within the Private View: A Note on Re-reading the Poetry of Edgar Allan Poe," *Partisan Review*, Vol. X (1943), 263–74.

for art's sake; . . . he stands at the exact point of transition between the Gothic romance, set in a haunted German castle, and that modern type of story in which the terror, as Poe said, "is not of Germany but of the soul"; and he stands at the exact point where Romantic Poetry is transformed into Symbolist Poetry.

Between 1949 and 1959, Allen Tate published several studies of Poe in which he discussed Poe's relationship to democracy, to nature, and to the cosmos and noted that Poe's greatest significance lies in his having been the origin of this century's great artistic theme, the disintegration of personality.

But the actual emphases that Poe gives the perversions are richer in philosophical implication than his psychoanalytic critics have been prepared to see. . . . Poe's symbols refer to a known tradition of thought . . . and are not merely the index to a compulsive neurosis; and . . . the symbols . . . point towards this larger philosophical dimension."[11]

T. S. Eliot issued four statements on Poe between 1927 and 1953. The first was a review of Allen's *Israfel* in *Nation and Athenaeum* in 1927.

Poe was not only an heroically courageous critic—the element of malice and irritability subtracted, there re-

[11] "The Angelic Imagination: Poe and the Power of Words," *Kenyon Review*, Vol. XIV (1952), 455–75; other studies by Tate are "Our Cousin, Mr. Poe," *Partisan Review*, Vol. XVI (1949), 1207–19, and "Three Commentaries: Poe, James, and Joyce," *Sewanee Review*, Vol. LVIII (1950), 1–15. *The Forlorn Demon* (Chicago, 1953) reprinted "Our Cousin, Mr. Poe" and added "The Angelic Imagination: Poe as God." *Collected Essays* (Denver, 1959) includes all the essays from *The Forlorn Demon*.

mains a large part of his criticism which must be applauded for pure pluck—but a critic of the first rank. The men whom he attacked are utterly insignificant. Poe not only performed a service to literature in America by exterminating these pests, but incidentally wrote some masterly criticism.

Eliot's *From Poe to Valéry* appeared as a small book in 1948 and as an article in *The Hudson Review* the following year. In his review of *Israfel*, Eliot had said that even with the correction of biographical inaccuracies, "Poe remains inscrutable." In *From Poe to Valéry*, Eliot admitted that Poe is "a stumbling block for critics."

If we examine his work in detail, we seem to find in it nothing but slipshod writing, puerile thinking unsupported by wide reading or profound scholarship, haphazard experiments in various types of writing, chiefly under pressure of financial need, without perfection in any detail. This would not be just. But if, instead of regarding his work analytically, we take a distant view of it as a whole, we see a mass of unique shape and impressive size to which the eye constantly returns.

Having referred to the puzzling nature of Poe's influence—Eliot himself not sure whether or how much Poe's poetry influenced his own—and to a "certain flavour of provinciality" in Poe's work, Eliot argued, with specific illustrations from the poems, that Poe's poetry is incantatory verse, whose effect is "immediate and undeveloping," a kind of poetry which does not yield "a richer melody, through study and long habituation." Eliot considered Poe to be a powerful intellect but "the intellect of a highly gifted young person before puberty . . . a man of very exceptional mind and sensibility, whose emotional development has been in some respect arrested at an early age." Eliot agreed with Huxley that the French overrated Poe because their knowledge of English was imperfect, and he agreed with Cowley that Baudelaire transformed "a slipshod and a shoddy English prose into admirable French." The French poets, however, beginning with Baudelaire, found in Poe the prototype of *le poete maudit* and in his verse an early example of *la poésie pure*. The *art poétique* which bore fruit in the work of Valéry germinated in the work of Poe.[12]

Eliot repeated his observation regarding Poe's influence on the symbolists and, subsequently, on twentieth-century verse, in *Notes Towards a Definition of Culture* in 1949.

> In the final years of the eighteenth century and the first quarter of the nineteenth, the Romantic movement in English poetry certainly dominated. But in the second half of the nineteenth century the greatest contribution to European poetry was certainly made in France. I refer to the tradition which starts with Baudelaire and culminates in Paul Valéry. I venture to say that without this French tradition the work of three poets in other languages—and three very different from each other—I refer to William Butler Yeats, to Rainer Maria Rilke, and, if I may, to myself—would hardly be conceivable. And, so complicated are these literary influences, we must remember that this French movement itself owed a good deal to an American of Irish extraction: Edgar Allan Poe.[13]

But if Eliot in 1948 leaned toward a measure of Poe as a "slipshod" writer and "puerile" thinker, albeit his influence

[12] *From Poe to Valéry.*
[13] Page 115.

on symbolism, he seems to have modified his attitude in an address which he delivered at Washington University in St. Louis on June 9, 1953: "American Literature and the American Language." Eliot identified as a landmark of a national literature that which combines "the strong local flavour . . . with unconscious universality." Writers like Thoreau, Emerson, Hawthorne, and Frost were local writers, said Eliot, more representative of New England than the whole of the American nation.

> The landmarks I have chosen for the identification of American literature are not found in New England. . . . The three authors of my choice are Poe, Whitman and Mark Twain. . . .
>      . . . Perhaps all that one can say of Poe is that his was a type of imagination that created its own dream world; that anyone's dream world is conditioned by the world in which he lives; and that the real world behind Poe's fancy was the world of Baltimore and Richmond and Philadelphia that he knew.[14]

And so it goes. The century began with a statement from Howells, who, once he had reconsidered his view of Poe after Emerson's dismissal of him as a "jingle-man," ventured to suggest Poe's name might some day lead all the rest among American immortals. Lawrence's diagnosis of Poe's work as a display of the disintegration of his psyche led Krutch and Marie Bonaparte to their conclusion that Poe's work is a re-creation of his neuroses rather than the product of a great imagination. Perfectly wrought but dead, said Hemingway, while Huxley protested, not the content, but the form of his poetic achievement. Quinn's biography

14 *To Criticize the Critic,* 52–54.

restored the human element to the Poe legend, and while Winters proclaimed Poe to be a writer of obvious crudity, Gregory, Cowley, and Tate found him to be, historically and permanently, a writer of some significance. Parrington thought Poe to be outside the current of American thought. Eliot, in conclusion, said that behind Poe's fancy was the real world he had known, and though he was willing to concede Poe's importance in the history of criticism and observed the need to take a distant view of his work as a whole, Eliot, nevertheless, left the impression that he considered Poe's content immature and his form imperfect.

Will Poe indeed lead the immortals, as Howells predicted, or will he at least, as Eliot noted, remain one of our most representative writers? Will his death recorded by Hemingway's obituary prove to be premature? Or will his work, which Tate said was the origin of the modern personality of literature, continue to hold its own along with that body of work in our time which he influenced? Part Two is one more attempt to see Poe's work "whole," as Eliot said the French have viewed it, and to examine it in view of a unified philosophy of thought whose conclusive expression came to be realized in *Eureka*.

# Eureka *and "The Raven": A Study in Unity*

# Introduction

ELIOT'S ACCEPTANCE OF POE as a forerunner of the symbolists and Tate's recognition of Poe's work as the origin of the modern personality in literature realize the prophecy made in the nineteenth century by the French: "Here is the literature of the twentieth century," wrote the Goncourts in their *Journals*. Such recognition, important as it is for Poe, establishes his relationship to European culture but leaves him out of American tradition. Was Poe so completely outside the current of American thought as Parrington and others have believed? Or was he not as close to that most important tradition—that which derives from Emerson—as were Thoreau and Whitman and Dickinson and Twain?

Eliot advocated viewing the work of Poe "whole," as the French did. Baudelaire and Valéry viewed the work of Poe whole, and they read and liked *Eureka*, which Poe considered his final expression. American readers of Poe took no notice of *Eureka* until recently, and if they did, it was only to consider it as a kind of curious afterthought—the kind of thing to expect from an eccentric nature like Poe—which was only vaguely related, if at all, to the work which had preceded it and not at all related to other literature produced in America at that time. None saw beyond the Gothic appearances of Poe's verses and fiction the same union of

47

realities which had produced "The Raven," "The Fall of the House of Usher," and *Eureka*. None saw that the philosophy of *Eureka* was basically the same pantheistic approach which had produced Emerson's "The Over-Soul." But then Emerson's essay is not always treated as the climactic expression in his pursuit of a transcendental philosophy. To be transcendental, according to popular belief, is to be self-reliant; there the emphasis is, and there it often ends. But self-reliance is only the momentary realization of truth on earth. Truth and creation had their beginning in an Over-Soul, and they are destined ultimately to a reunion with the Over-Soul.

Poe felt no fondness for Emerson, calling him a mystic for mysticism's sake and a lover of the obscure. Nevertheless, Poe's final truth, expressed in *Eureka*, was anticipated by Emerson's "The Over-Soul," published in *Essays, First Series*, in 1841, seven years before *Eureka*. The Over-Soul, Emerson's pantheistic term for God, is "that great nature in which we rest as the earth lies in the soft arms of the atmosphere; that Unity, that Over-Soul, within which every man's particular being is contained and made one with all other." This divine unity divides itself into parts which man identifies as the various aspects of creation but which in their relationship each to each retain their existence as a divine whole.

> *We live in succession, in division, in parts, in particles.* Meantime within man is the soul of the whole; the wise silence; the universal beauty, to which every part and particle is equally related; the eternal One. And this deep power in which we exist and whose beatitude is all accessible to us, is not only self-sufficing and perfect in every hour, but the act of seeing and the thing seen, the seer and the spectacle, the subject and the object, are one.

48

We see the world piece by piece, as the sun, the moon, the animal, the tree; but the whole, of which these are the shining parts, is the soul.

The divine stream manifests itself in man as his "wisdom and virtue and power and beauty." Philosophers and poets receive their truths from "an influx of the Divine mind" into their minds. Theirs are "perceptions of the absolute law." Divine revelation is in the mind of man, and the man who would know "what the great God speaketh" must withdraw from "the accents of other men's devotion" and "greatly listen to himself." Self-reliance once achieved, Emerson concluded, man "will weave no longer a spotted life of shreds and patches, but he will live with a divine unity."

And this because the heart in thee is the heart of all; not a wall, not an intersection is there anywhere in nature, but one blood rolls uninterruptedly an endless circulation through all men, as the water of the globe is all one sea, and, truly seen, its tide is one.

It is not so much the province of the following chapters to show the relationship between Emerson and Poe but rather to demonstrate that so much of what Poe wrote in *Eureka* he had been saying all along, in his poems and his short stories and, to some extent, in his criticism also. *Eureka*, like "The Over-Soul," is an important precursory document, in American literature at least, in anticipation of the Bergsonian, cyclical interpretation of man's evolution, which, infused with the doctrines of Spengler and Frazer, became one of the intellectual currents of the twentieth century.

# Eureka

POE READ *Eureka* as a two-hour public lecture at the Society Library in New York City on the evening of February 3, 1848. The audience was kept small by a stormy winter night, but the reading was favorably reported by the newspapers. *Eureka* was published in June of that same year, Poe having received from George Putnam an advance of fourteen dollars.

From biographical evidence we know that Poe attached great importance to the thought he expressed in *Eureka*. To Mrs. Clemm, on July 7, 1849, he wrote: "I have no desire to live since I have done *Eureka*. I could accomplish nothing more."[1] If he had been struggling toward thoughtful expression, it is apparent from this statement that Poe thought that at last he had succeeded in producing something conclusive.

Putnam, the publisher of *Eureka*, recorded his account of Poe's visit to his office on the subject of its publication. A nervous and excited gentleman, wrote Putnam, approached him with "a glittering eye" and proposed a publication of "momentous interest," whose revelations would be of greater importance than Newton's discovery of gravitation. To satisfy the universal and intense attention which the book would certainly create, the publisher should set

[1] John Ward Ostrom (ed.), *Letters* of Edgar Allan Poe, II, 452.

aside all other enterprises and make this one book the business of his lifetime, beginning with an edition of fifty thousand. No other scientific event in the world's history, Poe insisted, would approach in importance the developments of this book. Putnam agreed to an edition of five hundred and softened the poet's disappointment with a small loan.[2]

In the opening paragraph of *Eureka*, Poe conveyed the seriousness with which he approached his subject. "It is with humility really unassumed—it is with a sentiment even of awe—that I pen the opening sentence of this work; for of all conceivable subjects, I approach the reader with the most solemn, the most comprehensive, the most difficult, the most august." After expressing his intention to write on all aspects of the material and spiritual universe, he added, "I shall be so rash, moreover, as to challenge the conclusions, and thus, in effect, to question the sagacity of many of the greatest and most justly reverenced of men." Had Poe appeared previously as a philosopher, like Emerson perhaps, such an announced intention might have been considered more seriously. But before a reading public accustomed to the thrills provided by tales of mystery and terror, it passed by almost unnoticed.

"My general proposition, then," Poe declared, "is this:— *In the Original Unity of the First Thing lies the Secondary Cause of All Things, with the Germ of their Inevitable Annihilation.*" To the result of this occurrence Poe applied Pascal's definition of the universe: "a sphere of which the center is everywhere, the circumference nowhere." Unity, which Poe also called oneness, is all that he predicated of the originally created matter, but he proposed to show that

[2] "Leaves from a Publisher's Letter-Book," *Putnam's Magazine*, Vol. IV, n.s. (Oct., 1869), 467–75.

*"this Oneness is a principle abundantly sufficient to account for the constitution, the existing phenomena, and the plainly inevitable annihilation, of at least the Material Universe."*

Poe's thesis of creation and its ultimate return to the state which antedates creation closely parallels Christian doctrine, but in scientific and material, not theological and personal, terms. But with one important difference. The constitution of the material universe, he wrote, "has been effected by *forcing* the originally and therefore normally *One* into the abnormal condition of *Many*." Creation is division, expansion, of the original *One*; the godhead creates of itself; creation is not an act independent of its own matter, as in Christian theology which teaches that God created man and all manner of nature, independently of His own matter. But in a manner resembling theological doctrine, Poe's argument anticipates a return of all that which has been created to a point of origin, whatever form creation may have assumed. "A diffusion from Unity, under the conditions, involves a tendency to return into Unity—a tendency ineradicable until satisfied. . . . The assumption of absolute Unity in the primordial Particle includes that of infinite divisibility. . . . Difference of kind, too, is easily conceived to be merely a result of differences in size and form, taken more or less conjointly."

After arguing that oneness has divided itself into countless diversities, Poe sought to illustrate the relationship of the many, each to each, perhaps with Emerson's "Each and All" in view at this point. "If I propose to ascertain the influence of one mote in a sunbeam on its neighboring mote, I cannot accomplish my purpose without first accounting and weighing all the atoms in the Universe, and defining the precise positions of all at one particular moment. . . .

Does not so evident a brotherhood among the atoms point to a common parentage? . . . In a word, is it not because the atoms were, at some remote epoch of time, even more than together—is it not because originally, and therefore normally, they were One—that now, in all circumstances, at all points, in all directions, by all modes of approach, in all relations and through all conditions they struggle back to this absolutely, this irrelatively, this unconditionally *One*?" Original unity, Poe concluded, is the source of universal phenomena.

Poe interjected a rhetorical question at this point, and his answer serves to depersonalize the relationship man commonly assigns to himself and God and to the eventual reunion between them also. "The atoms, now, having been diffused from their normal condition of Unity, seek to return to—what? Not to any particular *point*, certainly. . . . It is merely the condition, not the point or locality at which the condition took its rise, that these atoms seek to reestablish; it is merely that condition which is their normality that they desire." Many a contemporary attitude was anticipated in *Eureka*; note this early expression of an existential attitude. The indifference of Creator to creation here described by Poe is certainly in tune with the teachings of Sartre. "The Thought of God is to be understood as originating the Diffusion—as proceeding with it—as regulating it—and, finally, as being withdrawn from it on its completion. Then commences Reaction, and through Reaction, 'Principle,' as we employ the word. It will be advisable, however, to limit the application of this word to the two immediate results of the discontinuance of the Divine Volition—that is, to the two agents, *Attraction* and *Repulsion*." These two agents characterize all existing phenomena between creation and return to unity. Poe defined attraction as gravity: *"Every atom, of every body, attracts every other atom, both of its own and of every other body,* with a force which varies inversely as the squares of the distances of the attracting and attracted atom." Regarding repulsion, "In fact, while the tendency of the diffused atoms to return into Unity will be recognized, at once, as the principle of the Newtonian Gravity, what I have spoken of as a repulsive influence prescribing limits to the (immediate) satisfaction of the tendency, will be understood as that which we have been in the practice of designating now as heat, now as a magnetism, now as electricity." The two forces, then, attraction and repulsion or gravity and electricity, operate against each other; while one seeks to return to the primordial unity, the other seeks to delay that return.

Apparently realizing that unanswered questions would now begin to arise in the reader's mind, Poe felt it necessary to interpolate: "I have taken it for granted, simply that the Beginning had nothing behind it or before it, that it was a Beginning in fact, that it was a Beginning and nothing different from a Beginning; in short, that this Beginning was—*that which it was.* If this be a 'mere assumption,' then a 'mere assumption' let it be." The relationship between gravity and the atomic beginning he emphasized as follows: *"The Law which we call Gravity exists on account of Matter's having been radiated, at its origin, atomically, into a limited sphere of Space, from one individual, unconditional, irrelative, and absolute Particle Proper, by the sole process in which it was possible to satisfy, at the same time, the two conditions—Radiation and equable distribution throughout the sphere."*

Poe continued to make assumptions, chose even to speculate, and in the following statement offered an indirect apology for what may seem unclear to some and untrue to others: "In the conduct of this Discourse I am aiming less at physical than at metaphysical order." Poe insisted that matter was diffused by determinate rather than by infinitely continued force. "Supposing a continuous force, we should be unable, in the first place, to comprehend a reaction at all; and we should be required in the second place to entertain the impossible conception of an infinite extension of matter." Poe wished to impress upon the reader, he said, the "certainty of there arising, at once (on withdrawal of the diffusive force, or Divine Volition), out of the condition of the atoms as described, at innumerable points throughout the universal sphere, innumerable agglomerations, characterized by innumerable specific differences of force, size, essential nature, and distance each from each. The development of Repulsion (Electricity) must have commenced, of course, with the very earliest particular efforts at Unity." If we divest ourselves of prejudice, Poe wrote, and by prejudice he could mean only traditional religious convictions, we "cannot fail to arrive, in the end, at the condensation of laws into Law—cannot fail of reaching the conclusion that *each law of Nature is dependent at all points upon all other laws*, and that all are but consequences of one primary exercise of the Divine Volition."

One of Poe's most interesting hypotheses is one which he admitted to be pure fancy. It is one about which the present world is certainly more curious than Poe's period was. "Let me declare, only, that, as an individual, I myself feel impelled to *fancy*—without daring to call it more— that there *does* exist a *limitless* succession of universes, more or less similar to that of which *alone* we shall ever have cognizance, at the very least until the return of our own particular Universe into Unity. *If* such clusters of clusters exist, however—*and they do*—it is abundantly clear that, having had no part in our origin, they have no portion in our laws. They neither attract us, nor we them. Their material, their spirit, is not ours—is not that which obtains in any part of our Universe. They could not impress our senses or our souls. Among them and us—considering all, for the moment, collectively—there are no influences in common. Each exists, apart and independently, in the bosom of its proper and particular God." Poe accepted the possibility of there being more than one God. There is a God, a source of creation, for each universe, each in its own time, presumably, due to return to the divine volition which diffused it into being.

Until recently the statement in *Eureka* which has interested commentators most in this work's relation to all of Poe's work is that in which Poe commended the Creator for "the absolute accuracy of the Divine *adaptation.*" Critics have already witnessed a parallel between this "absolute accuracy" and Poe's principles of composition. "The plots of God are perfect," Poe wrote in *Eureka*. "The Universe is a plot of God." So, it has been said, Poe attempted in art an imitation of the "Divine adaptation," viewing the artist as a god in miniature, who, if he follows the principles outlined by Poe, strives for a unity of effect and develops all elements, all words, in accord with the chosen effect, each related to the other and attracted to their center for, as Emerson said, a "perfect whole." At any rate, Poe concluded his description of this plot of God as follows: "Let us understand each star, with its attendant planets—as but a Titanic atom existing in space with precisely the same inclination for Unity which characterized, in the beginning, the actual atoms after their radiation throughout the Universal Sphere. As these original atoms rushed towards each other in generally straight lines, so let us conceive as at least generally rectilinear the paths of the system-atoms towards their respective centres of aggregation; and in this direct drawing together of the systems into clusters, with a similar and simultaneous drawing together of the clusters themselves while undergoing consolidation, we have at length attained the great *Now*—the awful Present—the Existing Condition of the Universe."

Having determined, to his satisfaction at least, the existing condition of the universe, Poe proceeded to an analysis of matter. "With a perfectly legitimate reciprocity, we are now permitted to look at Matter; . . . we are able to perceive Matter as a Means, not an end. Its purposes are thus seen to have been comprehended in its diffusion; and with the return into Unity these purposes cease. The absolutely consolidated globe of globes would be *objectless*; therefore not for a moment could it continue to exist. Matter, created for an end, would unquestionably, on fulfillment of that end, be Matter no longer. Let us endeavor to understand that it would disappear, and that God would remain all in all; . . . we are justified in assuming that Matter exists only as Attraction and Repulsion; in other words, that Attraction and Repulsion are Matter. . . . When, on fulfillment of its purposes, then, Matter shall have returned into its original condition of One . . . when, I say, Matter, finally, expelling the Ether, shall have returned into absolute Unity, it will then . . . be Matter without Attraction and without Repulsion—in other words, Matter without Matter—in other words, again, *Matter no more.*"

For purposes of this book, this last statement seems the most important of all. The diffusion of atoms into matter, Poe has argued, can result only in a return to their source of origin. Return can mean only the dissolution of matter, its having ceased to exist, its reasons for existence no more, since its absorption into a new condition supposes an identity between what was matter and the Divine Will. "On the Universal agglomeration and dissolution, we can readily conceive that a new and perhaps totally different series of conditions may ensue; another creation and radiation, returning into itself; another action and reaction of the Divine Will."

But the destruction of matter—its present condition no more, as its qualifying characteristics vanish—is by no means the end of the argument, for Poe contemplated a far more romantic conclusion. In its dissolution matter returns to what Poe was then prepared to call the "Heart Divine." In answer to his own rhetorical question, "This Heart Divine—what is it?" he replied dramatically, "It is our own." Justifiably, he maintained, "No thinking being lives who, at some luminous point of his life of thought, has not felt himself lost amid the surges of futile efforts at understanding or believing that anything exists *greater than his own soul.* The utter impossibility of any one's soul feeling itself inferior to another, the intense, overwhelming dissatisfaction and rebellion at the thought; these with the omniprevalent aspirations at perfection, are but the spiritual, coincident with the material, struggles toward the original Unity; are to my mind at least, a species of proof far surpassing what Man terms demonstration, that no one soul *is* inferior to another; that nothing is, or can be, superior to any one soul; that each soul is, in part, its own God—its own Creator; in a word, that God—the material *and* spiritual God—now exists solely in the diffused Matter and Spirit of the Universe; and that the regathering of this diffused Matter and Spirit will be but the re-constitution of the *purely* spiritual and individual God." What Poe began as a scientific treatise yields here to metaphysical terminology.

In this romantic conclusion whereby matter returns to its beginning and arrives finally at a state of perfection in unity, Poe found the justification for all the ills which attend life, which attend matter. "In this view, and in this view alone, we comprehend the riddles of Divine Injustice —of inexorable Fate. In this view alone the existence of Evil becomes intelligible; but in this view it becomes more —it becomes endurable. Our souls no longer rebel at a *sorrow* which we ourselves have imposed upon ourselves, in furtherance of our own purposes—with a view, if even with a futile view—to the extension of our own Joy." A century later T. S. Eliot re-examined the problem of human suffering, but unlike Poe, he settled for a view more religiously orthodox.

Poe's concluding statements assume a personal attitude toward the Creator. Specifically Poe referred to God, to Him, whereas earlier in the essay more commonly he referred to "Beginning" or "Original Unity" or the unparticled. "Those inconceivably numerous things designated as His Creatures," Poe wrote, "are really but infinite individualizations of Himself." All matter has become "His creatures," and to both animate and inanimate life Poe assigned the same sentient response. Both Nerval and Baudelaire recognized this argument as their own. Here is the axis on which turns all of French symbolism, which Nerval and Baudelaire compressed so well in their pioneering sonnets, "Vers Dorés" and "Correspondances."

And so *Eureka* concludes with an analogy between the animate life and the inanimate, the logic on which rests symbolism as a poetic technique. To the casual eye the symbol may seem far distant from the object of its association, but to the discerning mind relationships are everywhere because all manner of existence originate from the same source and belong, therefore, to the same identity. Here Poe elaborated upon an observation made some years earlier in "The Island of the Fay," published in *Graham's* in 1841. In a sketch devoted to the happiness to be experienced in contemplation of natural scenery, he warned that "we are madly erring, through self-esteem, in believing man, in either his temporal or future destinies, to be of more moment in the universe than that vast 'clod of the valley' which he tills and contemns, and to which he denies a soul for no more profound reason than that he does not behold it in operation."

All these creatures—*all*—those whom you term animate, as well as those to which you deny life for no better reason than that you do not behold it in operation—all these creatures have, in a greater or less degree, a capacity for pleasure and for pain; *but the general sum of their sensations is precisely that amount of Happiness which appertains by right to the Divine Being when concentrated within Himself*. These creatures are all, too, more or less, and more and less obviously, conscious Intelligences; conscious, first, of a proper identity; conscious, secondly, and by faint indeterminate glimpses, of an identity with the Divine Being of whom we speak—of an identity with God. Of the classes of consciousness, fancy that the former will grow weaker, the latter stronger, during the long succession of ages which must elapse before these myriads of individual Intelligences become blended—when the bright stars become blended—into One. Think that the Sense of individual identity will be gradually merged in the general consciousness; that Man, for example, ceasing imperceptibly to feel himself Man, will at length attain that awfully triumphant epoch when he shall recognize his existence as that of Jehovah. In the meantime bear in mind that all is Life—Life—Life within Life—the less within the greater, and all within the Spirit Divine.

Poe did not avoid a confusion common to all pantheistic argument. Wordsworth, Emerson, Whitman, and Bergson also provoked questions which they left unanswered. It is not the province of this work to discuss the accuracy of Poe's principles in the light of atomic discoveries made in the twentieth century, nor is it to determine who and to what extent were the influences upon Poe's thought.[3] For the most part, Poe dealt in generalities, and how much truth is to be found in them can be determined only by each individual for himself within the context of related beliefs. That Poe realized he might be less scientific than metaphysical and poetic he himself suggested in his Preface wherein he dedicated his work "to those who feel rather than to those who think—to the dreamers and those who put faith in dreams as the only realities." He wanted *Eureka* to be considered "as an Art-Product alone . . . as a Romance . . . as a Poem."

Poe's declaration on the nature of *Eureka* in its Preface offers a clue to an understanding of the work: "Nevertheless it is as a Poem only that I wish this work to be judged after I am dead." The opinion offered here is that Poe considered *Eureka* to be the climax to all the poetry he had written, not for its effect or its rhythms or its tone—for the

[3] For an analysis of the scientific principles in *Eureka* and a study of its sources, see Frederick W. Conner, *Cosmic Optimism; A Study of the Interpretation of Evolution by American Poets from Emerson to Robinson.* Conner observes that Poe's principal sources were Newton and Laplace and that Poe reduced both God and nature to the mechanical, whereas to Emerson, God did not cease to be transcendent and spiritual.

work is written entirely in prose and seems completely un-related to poetic content unless a parallel be drawn with Pope's *Essay on Man* or Eliot's *Four Quartets*—but rather for the climactic relationship which the thought of the work bears to the content of Poe's poetry.

The most revealing sentence of the Preface is one which is rarely quoted: "I offer this Book of Truths, not in its character of Truth-Teller, but for the Beauty that abounds in its Truth; constituting it true." As much as Poe may be indebted to Coleridge for his critical theories, the source, the inspiration, for this statement could have been none other than John Keats! When Keats wrote that "Beauty is Truth," he declared in effect that the second is indistin-guishable from the first because beauty is the source of truth and that art in giving permanence to beauty gives perma-nence to truth as well. To Poe death is part of that truth, an essential phase within the pattern of life. Beauty that must die—beauty "whose enjoyment is knowledge," to use Poe's phrase from "The Island of the Fay"—abounds in the truth of *Eureka*, wrote Poe, because the truth is not only life but "Life within Life," life or beauty within a larger, more perfect life and beauty, unrealizable except through death which makes possible the return from a state of diffusion to a reunion with the unparticled, the "Heart Divine."

T. S. Eliot's estimate of Poe as a thinker is that "there can be few authors of such eminence who have drawn so little from their own roots, who have been so isolated from any surroundings . . . the immature mind playing with ideas because it had not developed to the point of convictions."[4]

4 *From Poe to Valéry*, 9, 29. Later Eliot would express a change of mind regarding Poe's isolation from experience, in "American Litera-ture and the American Language," published in *To Criticize the Critic*.

viewed *Eureka* as "that cosmological fantasy which
      no deep impression upon most of us, because we are
aware of Poe's lack of qualification in philosophy, theology,
or natural science."[5]

That Poe did not use directly the materials of his experience in his verse and his fiction cannot be denied. The
content of Poe's work represents a complete transformation
of experience into meaning. The meaning he discovered in
reality he chose to relate in terms often unreal, in terms
not natural but supernatural. Not a philosopher or theo-
logian or scientist, Poe was an active participant in the
human experience, which taught him what became to him
the basic truth, influenced though he was by what he did
learn from those fields of learning in which, it has been
argued, he did not qualify! That basic truth he expounded
at length and with conclusive conviction in *Eureka*: that
man is diffused into an existence which can be only partly
joy and pleasure and that such existence is fated to disappear altogether, completely, for an eventual return to the
perfect state of being which he had known before diffusion.
The climax to his argument—the romantic reunion of
particle with the unparticled, of matter with its Creator,
of man with God—did not appear until *Eureka*, though
there were indications of Poe's interest in the nature of life
beyond the grave in earlier work.

Between 1839 and 1845, Poe published four "dialogues"
about the end of the world and the life beyond. In "The
Conversation of Eiros and Charmion" which appeared in
1839, Charmion, who has been dead for some time, welcomes Eiros to the realm of the dead, here called Aidenn—

[5] That Poe "did not know enough" was first advanced by Sidney
Lanier, long before Eliot; see *The Poems of Sidney Lanier* (New
York, 1884), xxxv–xxxvi.

"I rejoice to see you looking life-like and rational"—and asks him to describe earth's last hour before the comet struck and destroyed it.

> For a moment there was a wild lurid light alone, visiting and penetrating all things. Then let us bow down, Charmion, before the excessive majesty of the great God!— then, there came a shouting and pervading sound, as if from the mouth itself of HIM; while the whole incumbent mass of ether in which we existed, burst at once into a species of intense flame, for whose surpassing brilliancy and all-fervid heat even the angels in the high Heaven of pure knowledge have no name. Thus ended all.

"The Colloquy of Monos and Una," in 1841, describes the reunion of two lovers after death as "born again." Death had been the specter to check all human bliss. "That earnest mutual love, my own Monos, which burned within our bosoms—how vainly did we flatter ourselves, feeling happy in its first up-springing, that our happiness would strengthen with its strength! Alas! as it grew, so grew in our hearts the dread of that evil hour which was hurrying to separate us forever!" But "Mine, mine forever now!" exclaims Monos in joyous reply. The earth had been "art-scarred" and "intellect-scarred" because man "stalked a God in his own fancy," and an "infantile imbecility" overtook his reason because he accepted the idea of universal equality despite the "loud warning voice of the laws of gradation so visibly pervading all things in Earth and Heaven." Poe's conclusion at this point, spoken by Monos, was that "for the infected world at large I could anticipate no regeneration save in death. That man, as a race, should not become extinct, I saw that he must be born again."

"Mesmeric Revelation," published in 1844, Poe described

as a "colloquy occurring between a sleep-waker and my-self." Poe transcribed the man's replies to questions about God, the universe, and the relation of man to God. God is not spirit or matter as we know it but matter unparticled, which permeates and impels all things so that matter is itself God. God is the perfection of matter, and all created things are but the thoughts of God.

> To create individual, thinking beings, it was necessary to incarnate portions of the divine mind. Thus man is in-dividualized. Divested of corporate investiture, he were God. . . . Man thus divested would be God—would be unindividualized. But he can never be thus divested—at least never will be; else we must imagine an action of God returning upon itself—purposeless and futile action. Man is a creature. Creatures are thoughts of God. It is the nature of thought to be irrevocable.

"The Power of Words," which appeared in 1845, resumes the dialogue between reunited lovers in Aidenn after the final overthrow of the earth. This time Agathos welcomes Oinos, who asks if at last all things must be known. Final knowledge is the one thing unknown even to the Most High, says Agathos. In the beginning only the Deity cre-ated. The creatures which perpetually spring into being are "mediate and indirect," not direct and immediate re-sults of the divine creative power. Creation after the initial beginning is only motion, and "the source of all motion is thought, and the source of all thought is—God." By way of illustration, Agathos and Oinos moved their hands when they were dwellers on earth and gave vibration to the at-mosphere which in time resulted in the formation of a star.

Other statements of Poe's interest in the cosmos and the life of the spirit appeared in his letters and criticism. In a letter to Lowell, dated July 2, 1844, Poe said he had "no belief in spirituality" and that God is unparticled matter whose thought activity creates man as an individualization of the unparticled matter.[6] In his review of a book of essays by Macaulay, Poe expressed the belief that "all things are in a perpetual state of progress; that nothing in nature is perfect."[7]

But these miscellaneous expressions which led to *Eureka* are incomplete and inconclusive speculations. They offer faint contradiction to the despair and gloom which characterize Poe's major work. Before *Eureka* the emphasis in the poetry and in the best fiction is all on decay, disintegration, death; for life diffused into being combines the two opposing forces of attraction and repulsion, which produce decline and dissolution before death and the ultimate return. The longer Poe lived, the more experience intensified his impression of life as a process of loss and decomposition. Over and over again his poems and his stories reflect this impression. That he was able to resolve his despair into the romantic conclusion which is *Eureka* determines Poe as a romanticist more effectively than does his use of Gothic settings and supernatural occurrences or even the outpourings of his grieving heart.

[6] *Letters*, I, 256–58.
[7] Review of Macaulay's *Critical and Miscellaneous Essays*, in *Graham's Magazine*, June, 1841.

# "The Raven" and Other Poems

WHEN POE CRIED "Eureka" in 1848, he imposed a hopeful conclusion upon a body of work which, as a reflection of life, had until then received its most revealing description in the poem "The Conqueror Worm," first printed in 1843 in *Graham's* and afterward included in a revision of "Ligeia" in 1845 in the *Broadway Journal*.

> Lo! 'tis a gala night
>   Within the lonesome latter years!
> An angel throng, bewinged, bedight
>   In veils, and drowned in tears,
> Sit in a theatre, to see
>   A play of hopes and fears,
> While the orchestra breathes fitfully
>   The music of the spheres.
>
> Mimes, in the form of God on high,
>   Mutter and mumble low,
> And hither and thither fly—
>   Mere puppets they, who come and go
> At bidding of vast formless things
>   That shift the scenery to and fro,
> Flapping from out their Condor wings
>   Invisible Wo!
>
> That motley drama!—oh, be sure
>   It shall not be forgot!

With its Phantom chased forever more,
   By a crowd that seize it not,
Through a circle that ever returneth in
   To the self-same spot,
And much of Madness and more of Sin
   And Horror the soul of the plot.

But see, amid the mimic rout,
   A crawling shape intrude!
A blood-red thing that writhes from out
   The scenic solitude!
It writhes!—it writhes!—with mortal pangs
   The mimes become its food,
And the seraphs sob at vermin fangs
   In human gore imbued.

Out—out are the lights—out all!
   And over each quivering form,
The curtain, a funeral pall,
   Comes down with the rush of a storm,
And the angels, all pallid and wan,
   Uprising, unveiling, affirm
That the play is the tragedy, "Man,"
   And its hero the Conqueror Worm.

Biographical interpretation always associates the narrator with Poe, but it is Ligeia who speaks the poet's mind, not only in her verses but also most tellingly in her exclamation which follows the reading of her poem by the narrator.

"O God!" half shrieked Ligeia, leaping to her feet and extending her arms aloft with a spasmodic movement, as I made an end of these lines—"O God! O Divine Father!—shall these things be undeviatingly so?—shall this Conqueror be not once conquered? Are we not part and parcel in thee?"

It is not without protest, then, that Ligeia records her definition of life as a tragedy wherein death is the hero. But Poe would have no answer for her searching cries until after all his stories and his poems had been written—not until *Eureka,* in which he proclaims that the Conqueror has been vanquished, for man is indeed part and parcel of the Creator Himself.

How and when Poe reached the hopeful conclusion on which ended a career of despair and gloom cannot be known. No biographical evidence has so far turned up to determine how he evolved his conclusion. Had Poe lived longer, he might have written an essay entitled "How I Came To Write *Eureka,*" but no critic would have believed him! Certainly he was influenced by thinkers like Newton, La Place, Humboldt, Coleridge, Plato, and Emerson. Most of the work which preceded *Eureka* had as its theme the conquest of life by the Conqueror Worm. What became in *Eureka* the process by which creation returns to unity Poe had previously delineated as a spectacle of decomposition, an end in itself, seemingly without purpose. The climax to the despairing attitude which prevailed in his best work until *Eureka,* wherein it was reversed, was "The Raven," in 1845, three years before *Eureka.*

Critics continue to complain that "The Raven" is without very much meaning—"an elocutionist's display piece," as one critic again described it as late as 1962. For the meaning of "The Raven," if it is not sufficiently clear in the poem itself, Poe himself supplied at least a partial answer in his "Reply to the Letter of Outis" and in "The Philosophy of Composition." In the former Poe wrote, "In the concluding stanza, it is true, I suddenly convert him into an allegorical emblem of personification of Mournful Remembrance, out of which the poet is 'lifted nevermore.'" In the concluding paragraph of "The Philosophy of Composition," Poe referred to the raven as "emblematical—but it is not until the very last line of the very last stanza, that the intention of making him emblematical of Mournful and Never-Ending Remembrance is permitted distinctly to be seen." It is interesting that Poe referred to himself, the poet, as the hero of the poem, and his use of words like "emblem" and "personification" is interesting also. For today's reader such words spell "symbol."

The raven, then, according to the poet himself, symbolizes memory. It comes tapping at the poet's chamber door, and when the poet peers into the darkness, wondering, fearing, and whispers the word "Lenore," the silence remains unbroken except for the echo which murmurs back the word "Lenore."

1 Once upon a midnight dreary, while I pondered, weak and weary,
  Over many a quaint and curious volume of forgotten lore,
  While I nodded, nearly napping, suddenly there came a tapping,
  As of some one gently rapping, rapping at my chamber door,
  "Tis some visitor," I muttered, "tapping at my chamber door—

        Only this and nothing more."

2 Ah, distinctly I remember it was in the bleak December,
  And each separate dying ember wrought its ghost upon the floor,
  Eagerly I wished the morrow;—vainly I had sought to borrow
  From my books surcease of sorrow—sorrow for the lost Lenore—

For the rare and radiant maiden whom the angels name
Lenore—

> Nameless here for evermore.


5 And the silken, sad, uncertain rustling of each purple
curtain
Thrilled me—filled me with fantastic terrors never felt
before;
So that now, to still the beating of my heart, I stood
repeating;
" 'Tis some visitor entreating entrance at my chamber
door—
Some late visitor entreating entrance at my chamber
door;—

> This it is and nothing more."


4 Presently my soul grew stronger; hesitating then no
longer,
"Sir," said I, "or Madam, truly your forgiveness I implore;
But the fact is I was napping, and so gently you came
rapping,
And so faintly you came tapping, tapping at my chamber
door,
That I scarce was sure I heard you"—here I opened wide
the door;—

> Darkness there, and nothing more.


5 Deep into that darkness peering, long I stood there
wondering, fearing,
Doubting, dreaming dreams no mortals ever dared to
dream before;
But the silence was unbroken, and the stillness gave no
token,
And the only word there spoken was the whispered word,
"Lenore!"

This I whispered, and an echo murmured back the word,
  "Lenore!"—

Merely this and nothing more.

When the tapping resumes, the poet flings open the shutter, the door having yielded only darkness, and in comes "the stately Raven," which perches on the bust of Pallas and, upon being asked its name, answers only, "Nevermore!"

6Open here I flung the shutter, when, with many a flirt and flutter,
  In there stepped a stately raven of the saintly days of yore;
  Not the least obeisance made he; not a minute stopped or stayed he;
  But, with mien of lord or lady, perched above by chamber door—
  Perched above a bust of Pallas just above my chamber door—

Perched, and sat, and nothing more.

7Then this ebony bird beguiling my sad fancy into smiling,
  By the grave and stern decorum of the countenance it wore,
  "Though thy crest be shorn and shaven, thou," I said, "art sure no craven,
  Ghastly grim and ancient raven wandering from the Nightly shore—
  Tell me what thy lordly name is on the Night's Plutonian shore!"

Quoth the raven, "Nevermore."

8The poem takes its meaning from two questions which the poet then addresses to the bird: will he find refuge in heaven from the sorrows of earth and will he in the next life know again the "sainted maiden whom the angels name Lenore."

8 "Prophet!" said I, "thing of evil!—prophet still, if bird or devil!—
Whether Tempter sent, or whether tempest tossed thee here ashore,
Desolate, yet all undaunted, on this desert land enchanted—
On this home by Horror haunted,—tell me truly, I implore—
Is there—*is* there balm in Gilead?—tell me—tell me, I implore!"
Quoth the raven, "Nevermore."

9 "Prophet!" said I, "thing of evil!—prophet still, if bird or devil!
By that heaven that bends above us—by that God we both adore—
Tell this soul with sorrow laden if, within the distant Aidenn,
It shall clasp a sainted maiden whom the angels name Lenore—
Clasp a rare and radiant maiden whom the angels name Lenore."
Quoth the raven, "Nevermore."

The raven's answer to these questions is the same that it gives to the query about its name: "Nevermore." Memory, which is all that remains of past experience, has but one meaning to give: that which man has lost can never be restored to him. The answer to the first question—"*is* there balm in Gilead?"—becomes affirmative in *Eureka* with its theme of eventual return from diffusion to original unity.

But the return to a state of perfect unity with God does not include a reunion with the "sainted maiden." Lenore, therefore, becomes the symbol of all that is earthbound, of all experience associated with physical being. A few years before "The Raven," in his "Sonnet—Silence," Poe defined death as the "corporate Silence" whose name is "No More." He denied the Christian reunion of body and soul, as he affirmed only the reunion of soul with soul, man with God, the reunion of particled with the unparticled, a return to what T. S. Eliot has called "the Still Point." Destruction, then, is the theme of experience, as Poe saw it, and so it remained the theme of all his art, which is not so alienated from life after all. The artist professes to re-create life as he observes it, and if Poe did not in his verse and his short stories apply the cosmological romance which distinguishes *Eureka*, it was because the life of earthly experience does not contain it.

Two observations must be made regarding the objective content of "The Raven." The first concerns the raven itself. Why a raven? In an early draft Poe is supposed to have used an owl, traditional bird of wisdom associated with Athena. Why did he finally select a raven to reveal what he believed to be the final knowledge? In "The Philosophy of Composition," Poe explained that he considered first a parrot but forthwith substituted "a Raven, as equally capable of speech, and infinitely more in keeping with an intended tone." Much has been made of the association with Dickens' raven in *Barnaby Rudge*, but not much more can be said than that Dickens used the raven first. That Poe associated the raven with death is clear, not only from its message, "Nevermore," the meaning of which is death, but also from the poet's description of the bird and its origin. From the darkness comes the "ebony bird," the

"Ghastly, grim, and ancient Raven" from the "Night's Plutonian shore." Whatever Poe's motive may have been, his choice of the bird of death to deliver the message establishes a contrast with the dove, symbol of divine enlightenment contained in the Holy Ghost. To symbolize this life Poe chose an image of death because this life can only die, and this phase of his meaning he never changed. The joy in *Eureka* is really a triumph which results from a transformation of all matter into God, not from a recovery of the life known to earth. The raven, significantly, perches *above* the bust of Pallas, legendary goddess of wisdom, to profess that its wisdom is greater than all other, greater than all the knowledge contained in the books which line the poet's study. In "The Philosophy of Composition," Poe wrote, "I made the bird alight on the bust of Pallas . . . as most in keeping with the scholarship of the lover." In the poem the narrator cries: ". . . vainly I had sought to borrow/From my books surcease of sorrow." The knowledge which they offer, symbolized by Pallas, yields to the knowledge offered by the bird in its one-word wisdom, "Nevermore."

10. "Be that word our sign of parting, bird or fiend!" I
    shrieked, upstarting—
    "Get thee back into the tempest and the Night's
    Plutonian shore!
    Leave no black plume as a token of that lie thy soul hath
    spoken!
    Leave my loneliness unbroken!—quit the bust above my
    door!
    Take thy beak from out my heart, and take thy form from
    off my door!"

    Quoth the raven, "Nevermore."

11 And the raven, never flitting, still is sitting, *still* is sitting
   On the pallid bust of Pallas just above my chamber door;
   And his eyes have all the seeming of a demon's that is
      dreaming,
   And the lamp-light o'er him streaming throws his shadow
      on the floor;
   And my soul from out that shadow that lies floating on
      the floor

   Shall be lifted—nevermore!

In "The Philosophy of Composition," wherein Poe outlined how he came to write "The Raven," appears the
thesis advanced earlier in "The Poetic Principle": "Beauty
is the sole legitimate province of the poem." Poe explained,
not too convincingly, that "beauty of whatever kind, in its
supreme development, invariably excites the sensitive soul
to tears. Melancholy is thus the most legitimate of all
poetical tones." What is thus the most melancholy of
topics, he asked, and the answer is death. And when is this
topic most poetical? "When it most closely allies itself to
Beauty," he replied. Then he concluded that the death of
a beautiful woman is "unquestionably, the most poetical
topic in the world." When Poe reasoned that a poem is
best realized when it records a bereaved lover's complaint
for a dead beauty, it may be that again the poet's inspiration was Keats. The death of a beautiful woman unites
beauty with truth. While Keats chose as his subject beauty
in an arrested moment recorded on an urn, he decided,
nevertheless, as Poe would after him, that beauty inevitably
yields to its own destruction, that is, to its own final truth,
and in that moment when it does—in Poe's view—the two
become as one: beauty is truth. Poe's transfiguration of
"truth-beauty" became *Eureka*, which he prefaced with the

declaration, "What I here propound is true." Even as he argued for pure pleasure as the sole objective of a poem in "The Poetic Principle," Poe admitted that the "lessons of truth" might well invade upon a poem's contemplation of the beautiful.

If in "The Raven," Poe gave climactic utterance to his recognition of life as matter destined for disintegration, he had, almost from the beginning, though not with the same degree of finality, recorded the same truth. As early as "Tamerlane" (1827), he observed that

. . . all we live to know is known
And all we seek to keep hath flown—

In "A Dream within a Dream" (1827), he asked,

Is *all* that we see or seem
But a dream within a dream?

In "The Happiest Day, the Happiest Hour" (1827), he concluded he would not live again the brightest hour of the happiest day because "on its wing was dark alloy." In "The Lake: To ——" (1827), the "lone lake" assumes a symbolic reflection of the nightly pall which overtakes his soul, and there would be "in its gulf a fitting grave." If one accepts Professor Stovall's interpretation of "Al Aaraaf" (1829), Poe was thinking about the destruction of the world even then, though he seems to have limited its destruction in this poem to the crust of the orb alone.[1]

Among the early works, we find in the sonnet, "To Science" (1829), the most interesting correlation with *Eureka*. For if *Eureka* reversed the negative reply of the

[1] Floyd Stovall, "An Interpretation of Poe's 'Al Aaraaf,'" *Univ. of Texas Studies in English*, Vol. IX (1929), 106–33.

raven to the poet's question—whether there be balm in Gilead—it also provided a revision of the conviction expressed in "To Science."

Science! true daughter of Old Time thou art!
  Who alterest all things with thy peering eyes.
Why preyest thou thus upon the poet's heart,
  Vulture, whose wings are dull realities?
How should he love thee? or how deem thee wise?
  Who wouldst not leave him in his wandering
To seek for treasure in the jewelled skies,
  Albeit he soared with an undaunted wing?
Hast thou not dragged Diana from her car?
  And driven the Hamadryad from the wood
To seek a shelter in some happier star?
  Hast thou not torn the Naiad from her flood,
The Elfin from the green grass, and from me
The summer dream beneath the tamarind tree?

How should he deem science wise—science which has dragged Diana from her car and driven the Hamadryad from the wood! The "summer dream beneath the tamarind tree," torn from him by science in the early sonnet, is restored, though perhaps transformed as well, in *Eureka*, wherein science becomes the art of God, the creation, we might say, of *His* imagination. Thus the poet became reconciled to science, which in the beginning seemed but a destroyer, as even death he came to recognize as a phase of science as essential as the orbit of a planet. Science as the "true daughter . . . Who alterest all things" and "preyest . . . upon the poet's heart" became in *Eureka* the expression of God's diffusion into matter and the subsequent return of that matter to divine unity.

As early as 1831, as if in anticipation of many poems and

stories to follow, Poe wrote in an enlarged version of "Romance":

> For, being an idle boy lang syne,
> Who read Anacreon, and drank wine,
> I early found Anacreon rhymes
> Were almost passionate sometimes—
> And by strange alchemy of brain
> His pleasures always turn'd to pain—
> His naivete to wild desire—
> His wit to love—his wine to fire—
> And so, being young and dipt in folly
> I fell in love with melancholy,
> And used to throw my earthly rest
> And quiet all away in jest—
> I could not love except where Death
> Was mingling his with Beauty's breath—

In "Israfel," which also appeared as early as 1831, the poet lamented his "mortal melody" as he observed that Israfel himself "might not sing so wildly well" were he, like Poe, an inhabitant of earth.

> Yes, Heaven is thine; but this
>   Is a world of sweets and sours;
>   Our flowers are merely—flowers,
> And the shadow of thy perfect bliss
>   Is the sunshine of ours.
>
> If I could dwell
> Where Israfel
>   Hath dwelt, and he where I,
> He might not sing so wildly well
>   A mortal melody,
> While a bolder note than this might swell
>   From my lyre within the sky.

Poe's expressed dislike for allegory does not invalidate its presence in his work. The use of symbol, it has been repeatedly pointed out, can be an unconscious act. "The City in the Sea" (1831), it would seem, is Poe's representation of a civilization inundated by the waters of time.[2]

Lo! Death has reared himself a throne
In a strange city lying alone
Far down within the dim West,
Where the good and the bad and the worst and the best
Have gone to their eternal rest.
There shrines and palaces and towers
(Time-eaten towers that tremble not!)
Resemble nothing that is ours.
Around, by lifting winds forgot,
Resignedly beneath the sky
The melancholy waters lie.

No rays from the holy heaven come down
On the long night-time of that town;
But light from out the lurid sea
Streams up the turrets silently—
Gleams up the pinnacles far and free—
Up domes—up spires—up kingly halls—
Up fanes—up Babylon-like walls—
Up shadowy long-forgotten bowers
Of sculptured ivy and stone flowers—
Up many and many a marvellous shrine
Whose wreathed friezes intertwine
The viol, the violet, and the vine.

Resignedly beneath the sky
The melancholy waters lie.

[2] "The City in the Sea" first appeared as "The Doomed City" in 1831 and underwent several revisions before its final form in 1845, from which the lines quoted are taken.

So blend the turrets and shadows there
That all seem pendulous in air,
While from a proud tower in the town
Death looks gigantically down.

Ruins and memories blend as "turrets and shadows," and
the poet's resignation to the destruction of matter finds its
reflection in the refrain:

Resignedly beneath the sky
The melancholy waters lie.

Even closer to the truth of *Eureka* than "The City in the
Sea" is "The Coliseum" (1833). After weary pilgrimage
the poet comes to kneel before this "type of antique Rome,"
to feel, as "an altered and an humble man," the "grandeur,
gloom, and glory."

Type of the antique Rome! Rich reliquary
Of lofty contemplation left to Time
By buried centuries of pomp and power!
At length—at length—after so many weary days
Of weary pilgrimage and burning thirst
(Thirst for the springs of lore that in thee lie),
I kneel, an altered and an humble man,
Amid thy shadows, and so drink within
My very soul thy grandeur, gloom, and glory!

The lines which excite the most are those which prophesy
the poet's rejection of a Christian creation and resurrection.

Vastness! and Age! and Memories of Eld!
Silence! and Desolation! and dim Night!
I feel ye now—I feel ye in your strength—

O spells more sure than e'er Judaean King
Taught in the gardens of Gethsemane!

The stones have "spells" to cast more significant than the teachings of Christ.

Prophetic sounds and loud arise forever
From us, and from all Ruin, unto the wise,
As melody from Memnon to the Sun.
We rule the hearts of mightiest men—we rule
With a despotic sway all giant minds.
We are not impotent—we pallid stones.
Not all our power is gone—not all our fame—
Not all the magic of our high renown—
Not all the wonder that encircles us—
Not all the mysteries that in us lie—
Not all the memories that hang upon
And cling around about us as a garment,
Clothing us in a robe of more than glory.

The phrase "prophetic sounds" makes it clear that the poet had more in mind than a mere evocation of past glory. Man and his creations are both doomed to ruin, both uttering the same prophetic truth! All existence, even the most glorious, is "a dream within a dream," destined to decay and disappear as diffusion yields to the returning process.

After "The Raven," Poe's poems continued to express the decay of reality as their theme—in "Ulalume" (1847), in "Eldorado" (1849), in "Annabel Lee" (1849), in "The Bells" (1849). "The Raven" and "Ulalume" relate the same story and reach the same conclusion. In "Ulalume" the poet, with tears on his cheeks, follows Psyche, his soul, as she guides him through the "ghoul-haunted woodland of Weir."

The skies they were ashen and sober;
    The leaves they were crisped and sere—
    The leaves they were withering and sere;
It was night in the lonesome October
    Of my most immemorial year;
It was hard by the dim lake of Auber,
    In the misty mid region of Weir—
It was down by the dank tarn of Auber,
    In the ghoul-haunted woodland of Weir.

Here once, through an alley Titanic,
    Of cypress, I roamed with my Soul—
    Of Cypress, with Psyche, my Soul.
These were days when my heart was volcanic
    As the scoriac rivers that roll—
    As the lavas that restlessly roll
Their sulphurous currents down Yaanek
    In the ultimate climes of the pole—
That groan as they roll down Mount Yaanek
    In the realms of the boreal pole.

Psyche distrusts the light cast by the luminous Astarte beaming upon them "with Hope and in Beauty." The poet pacifies Psyche and strives to tempt her out of her gloom until they are stopped "by the door of a tomb—/By the door of a legended tomb."

And I said: "What is written, sweet sister,
    On the door of this legended tomb?"
    She replied: "Ulalume—Ulalume—
    Tis the vault of thy lost Ulalume!"

The role of the raven is taken here by Psyche, who upon being asked what is written on the door of the tomb, replies, "Ulalume," as the raven before her replied, "Nevermore." Astarte, who symbolizes the dream man associates with his future, beams with hope and beauty and, it would seem, points out the path to the "Lethean peace of the skies," while all the time it leads man but to the ghoul-haunted woodland of death.

> Then my heart it grew ashen and sober
>> As the leaves that were crisped and sere—
>> As the leaves that were withering and sere;
> And I cried; "It was surely October
>> On *this* very night of last year
>> That I journeyed—I journeyed down here!—
>> That I brought a dread burden down here—
>> On this night of all nights in the year,
>> Ah, what demon has tempted me here?
> Well I know, now, this dim lake of Auber—
>> This misty mid region of Weir—
> Well I know, now, this dank tarn of Auber,
>> This ghoul-haunted woodland of Weir."

It may be that the "Lethean peace of the skies" is a prophecy of the peace of *Eureka,* achieved through the cosmological reunion of man with God which follows death. As they relate to lost love and all lost reality, the words "Ulalume" and "Nevermore" contain the same symbolic message. Reality is but appearance. It cannot be again. In a letter to a lady who requested a copy of the poem because she had not understood it from Poe's reading the preceding night, Poe wrote that she would find "the verses scarcely more intelligible today in my manuscript than last night in my recitation" and then excused himself from explication with a reference to Dr. Johnson's remark about "the folly of explaining what, if worth explanation, should explain itself."[3]

[3] To Mrs. Susan Ingram, Norfolk, Va., September 10, 1849, in *Letters,* II, 460.

"Eldorado," which some have thought was inspired by the Gold Rush, contains the very same negative reply given to the poet by the raven and by Psyche. A bold and gallant knight bewails his failure to find Eldorado and seeks to learn from a "pilgrim shadow" where it can be found—"This land of Eldorado."

>  "Over the Mountains
>    Of the Moon,
>  Down the Valley of the Shadow,
>    Ride, boldly ride,"
>    The shade replied,—
>  "If you seek for Eldorado."

The answer remains "Nevermore," for Eldorado lies in the "Valley of the Shadow." Lenore will not return—she lies buried in the vault—and the knight who sings his song in search of Eldorado—perhaps the poet himself as he wrote verse after verse, story after story, and still did not find the fame and glory of his dreams—grew old, and still he found "No spot of ground/That looked like Eldorado." In another context of meaning, the "sunshine" and "shadow" of the third line may be references to this life and the next, and "Eldorado" a substitute for "Eureka." "Nevermore" and "Ulalume" yield in the development of Poe's thought to "Eureka" and "Eldorado" as symbols of man's reunion with eternity. As in "Monos and Una," the "gallant knight" who "grew old" and whose "strength/ Failed him at length" would be "born again" when he found Eldorado.

In "Annabel Lee," as in "The City in the Sea" and "The Coliseum," life has been engulfed by the sounding sea of time. The manifestation of matter which we call reality has become but a memory, a recall to what Poe in "Ulalume" calls the "love in her luminous eyes."

87

For the moon never beams without bringing me dreams
   Of the beautiful Annabel Lee;
And the stars never rise but I see the bright eyes
   Of the beautiful Annabel Lee;
And so, all the night-tide, I lie down by the side
Of my darling, my darling, my life and my bride,
   In her sepulchre there by the sea—
   In her tomb by the sounding sea.

Like Ulalume and Lenore, Annabel Lee lies in her tomb—
all three representative of beauty-reality having disappeared
forever into the sepulcher of memory.

In his promotion of Poe as a poet of ideas, Professor Stovall pointed out that the four bells described in "The Bells"
symbolize the four stages in the life of man. The silver bells
of youth become the golden bells of maturity, which in
time yield to the brazen fire bells that ring out of existence
the lust for life in old age, after which finally the iron bells
toll the funereal exit of man. The king of the ghouls who
tolls the iron bells is Death himself as Poe captures here
the spirit of a *danse macabre*.

Hear the tolling of the bells—
     Iron bells!
What a world of solemn thought their monody compels!
   In the silence of the night,
   How we shiver with affright
At the melancholy menace of their tone!
   For every sound that floats
   From the rust within their throats
     Is a groan.
    And the people—ah, the people—
    They that dwell up in the steeple,
     All alone,
And who tolling, tolling, tolling,

In that muffled monotone,
Feel a glory in so rolling
    On the human heart a stone—
They are neither man nor woman—
They are neither brute nor human—
        They are Ghouls:—
And their king it is who tolls:—
And he rolls, rolls, rolls,
        Rolls
    A paean from the bells;
And his merry bosom swells
    With the paen of the bells!
And he dances, and he yells;
Keeping time, time, time,
In a sort of Runic rhyme,
        To the paean of the bells—
            Of the bells;
Keeping time, time, time,
In a sort of Runic rhyme,
    To the throbbing of the bells—
Of the bells, bells, bells,
    To the sobbing of the bells;
Keeping time, time, time,
    As he knells, knells, knells,
In a happy Runic rhyme,
    To the rolling of the bells—
Of the bells, bells, bells;—
    To the tolling of the bells—
Of the bells, bells, bells, bells,
        Bells, bells, bells,
To the moaning and the groaning of the bells.


So the years pass into eternity, as the particled return to their center, while Poe's bells toll the music of the spheres! "The Bells" appropriately ended Poe's career as a poet, for preoccupied as he was until then with the "Nevermore" theme, it was not until he wrote "The Bells" and, possibly, "Eldorado" that he came to realize in verse a reflection in sound and suggestion of the triumphant theme which concluded his career in *Eureka*. The theme remains death in "The Bells," but the imagery has changed since Ligeia wrote her verses. The Conqueror Worm, "blood-red thing that writhes" with its "vermin fangs/In human gore imbued," has now become a king whose "merry bosom swells /With the paean of the bells!" Bells sound the departure from earth to unity—"moaning" and "groaning" bells, it is true, but bells, nevertheless—as the "tragedy, 'Man,'" is played out as a "happy Runic rhyme," and a "world of solemn thought their monody compels."

# *Tales of the Grotesque*

## an̶

THE DECLINE AND DECA                                              n
Poe's fiction with the sar                                       ̶
nessed in his verse. Fictio
its very nature, is more re
Here and there, too, amor
which digress from the
much of Poe's work. But                    ̶ ̶ except for
"The Pit and the Pendulum" and "Eleonora" it is not to
be found in his best work. Almost all re-enact the horror and
terror which characterize what in "The Conqueror Worm"
the author called "the tragedy, 'Man.'"

The most significantly prophetic statement written by
Poe in his early fiction appears in "MS. Found in a Bottle"
(1833), a story which relates what this study considers the
allegorical destruction of a ship going down in a whirlpool.

> To conceive the horror of my sensations is, I presume,
> utterly impossible; yet a curiosity to penetrate the mys-
> teries of these awful regions predominates even over my
> despair, and will reconcile me to the most hideous aspect
> of death. It is evident that we are hurrying onward to
> some exciting knowledge—some never-to-be-imparted
> secret, whose attainment is destruction.

Here in a sentence is what would become the argument of

*Eureka*: destruction must precede the final knowledge. In his Preface to *Tales of the Grotesque and Arabesque,* Poe pointed out that the terror he was writing of was "not of Germany but of the soul." The stories which illustrate most convincingly the thesis of man's annihilation are "Ligeia," which Poe considered his finest tale,[1] and "The Fall of the House of Usher," which readers have made their favorite.

"Ligeia" (1838) can be viewed on several levels. As a tale of horror, examined for no further implication, it relates the death of Ligeia, the narrator's remarriage with Rowena, and the subsequent transformation of the dying Rowena into a physical reincarnation of Ligeia. The biographical interpretation for this story reached its climactic statement in Marie Bonaparte's story of Poe. Rowena represents both Mrs. Allan and Virginia, in whom Poe betrayed the mother, who, as Ligeia, avenges her husband's infidelity.[2] Roy P. Basler has discussed Ligeia's reincarnation as an expression of wish fulfillment in the deranged narrator's imagination.[3] Examined on yet another level, the story can be assigned an interpretation which establishes it as an important preliminary phase before *Eureka.*

A consideration of "Ligeia" must take into serious account the epigraph which Poe cites as a quotation from Joseph Glanvill and which he repeats more than once in the course of narration.

And the will therein lieth, which dieth not. Who knoweth the mysteries of the will, with its vigor? For God is but a great will pervading all things by nature of

[1] ". . . undoubtedly the best story I have written." Poe to Evert A. Duyckinck, January 8, 1846, in *Letters,* II, 309.

[2] Bonaparte, 233.

[3] *Sex, Symbolism, and Psychology in Literature* (New Brunswick, 1948).

its intentness. Man doth not yield himself to the angels, nor unto death utterly, save only through the weakness of his feeble will.

Without question, "Ligeia" ranks high as a tale of horror, and its biographically Freudian suggestions may be given a certain degree of validity. It is also a story with a meaning. We have Poe's word for it.

The beginning of "Ligeia" recalls in setting and tone the beginning of "The Raven." "Buried in studies of a nature more than all else adapted to deaden impressions of the outward world, it is by that sweet word alone—by Ligeia— that I bring before mine eyes in fancy the image of her who is no more." Through knowledge the narrator seeks relief from the sorrow invoked by the image of "her who is no more." Like "The Raven," "Ligeia" dwells on inevitable death. Surcease would not be forthcoming until *Eureka.*

In "Ligeia," Poe as the narrator reveals the truth of an observation recorded many times elsewhere but never so completely and emphatically as he would expound it later in *Eureka.* Man's feeble will, which does not die, yields to the reunion with the greater will of God. Gravity pulls matter into a reunion with original unity. What "Ligeia" illustrates is not personal reincarnation but the reincarnation of the life process itself. Until the final dissolution the diffusion of matter continues. Man dies, and another is born to replace him. Life repeats itself, only to die again like Ligeia, whose weakness of will yields "to the angels," followed by Rowena, who in death resembles Ligeia because she, too, must yield. Death always wears the same face; hence the obvious relationship between the verses composed by Ligeia and the story which the narrator unfolds.

> And the angels, all pallid and wan,
>   Uprising, unveiling, affirm
> That the play is the tragedy, "Man,"
>   And its hero, the Conqueror Worm.

Poe's statement that Ligeia's return was momentary and that it was as Rowena that she was buried gives support to this interpretation.[4] Rowena's death in the image of Ligeia is an expression of death as a recurrent event. But the narrative itself provides sufficient evidence for this interpretation in the repeated death and revival of Rowena. Not once only but several times she returns to life before her final collapse as Ligeia.

> Why shall I pause to recite how, time after time, until near the period of the grey dawn, this hideous drama of revivification was repeated, and how each terrific relapse was only into a sterner and apparently more irredeemable death?

The history of man as a narrative of recurrent death Poe condensed to one symbolic night.

Very similar to "Ligeia" in theme and story is Poe's earlier effort, "Morella" (1835). Morella dies in childbirth, and the narrator-husband afterwards loves the child even more than he loved the mother, until the child, too, dies and is laid in the tomb where no trace of Morella can be found.

> As she had foretold, her child—to which in dying she had given birth, and which breathed not until the mother breathed no more—her child, a daughter, lived. And she grew strangely in stature and intellect, and was the perfect resemblance of her who had departed, and I loved

[4] Poe to Philip Cooke, September 21, 1839, in *Letters*, I, 118.

her with a love more fervent than I had believed it possible to feel for any denizen of earth.

But, ere long, the heaven of this pure affection became
darkened, and gloom, and horror, and grief, swept over
it in clouds. . . .

And, as the years rolled away, and I gazed, day after
day, upon her holy, and mild, and eloquent face, and
pored over her maturing form, day after day did I discover
new points of resemblance in the child to her mother, the
melancholy and the dead. . . .

. . . But she died; and with my own hands I bore her to
the tomb; and I laughed with a long and bitter laugh as
I found no traces of the first, in the charnel where I laid
the second—Morella.

As a horror story, "Morella" is all dependent upon the
empty tomb when the second Morella is laid to rest. When
Morella died, her soul transmigrated to her child, "which
breathed not until the mother breathed no more." As in
"Ligeia," the truth which emerges is the rebirth of life in
succeeding generations. This, it would seem, is the extent
to which Poe believed in reincarnation. When no trace of
Morella can be found in the tomb, the reader is confronted
with the realization that all reality must die and disappear.
The oft-repeated drama Poe here confined to mother and
child, but Ligeia and Rowena reveal essentially the same
story, so well reduced to a meaning by Ligeia herself in the
verses composed before her death.

An angel throng, bewinged, bedight
    In veils, and drowned in tears,
Sit in a theatre, to see
    A play of hopes and fears,
While the orchestra breathes fitfully
    The music of the spheres.

"The Fall of the House of Usher" (1839) submits a meaning as tellingly allegorical as the meaning offered by "Ligeia." This time the narrator is not the hero; he is merely the observer of a phenomenon which again concentrates the truth of the cosmos in an isolated scene of Gothic mansion and two principals. Madness and sin and horror are again the "soul of the plot," as Ligeia describes the "motley drama" in the third of her verses. In the fall of the House of Usher, Poe re-created in miniature the destruction of a dynasty, a civilization, even the whole world of reality as he came to envision the dissolution of all matter preceding the ultimate return to the "still point" of origin. The death of Roderick Usher and his sister Madeline, followed by the destruction of the house itself, produces an analogy of circumstance with the mortality imposed upon the first man and woman, followed by the expulsion from Eden. Roderick and Madeline perish, in the words of Ligeia, like mere puppets that come and go, and the house also, "At bidding of vast formless things/That shift the scenery to and fro."

Whether all these parallels were planted deliberately by Poe is unknown. More than likely, some of them were the result of subconscious creation, no more deliberate than the psychological parallels with his own experiences. Yet both are there, and the intellectual relationship of his poems and his stories to his ideas as they reached their conclusion in *Eureka* cannot be overemphasized. Poe's insistence that the purpose of art is pleasure, not truth, may obscure for a time a recognition of the idea. His reference to "truth" in "The Poetic Principle" is a reference to truth in didactic poetry. His use of the word "truth" may not have been wise, and though he elaborated with words like "moral" and "duty," it is the word "truth" which sticks in the mind. "All allegories are contemptible," Poe declared.[5] But Edward Davidson is correct when he observes that "Poe was an allegorist in spite of himself."[6]

An interesting example of a short story by Poe as allegory akin to his theme of disintegration and death is "The Cask of Amontillado" (1846). Ironically named Fortunato, the victim is a connoisseur of wine, the symbol here of the pleasure which life pursues, for it is the wine which entices Fortunato into the vault and to his subsequent death. The narrator is Death himself, playing here the role taken by Astarte in "Ulalume," leading his victim on with a smile— "my smile was now at the thought of his immolution." The time is dusk, "during the supreme madness of the carnival season," and Fortunato's appearance is that of the traditional fool wearing "a tight-fitting parti-stripped dress" and the "conical cap and bells." Fortunato's journey through the vaults, as he hurries on his way to judge the "wine," is interrupted by his coughing, which he relieves with wine from bottles shelved along their path. "The wine sparkled in his eyes and the bells jingled. . . . 'I drink,' he said, 'to the buried that repose around us.' " He and Death pass through a range of low arches, descend, pass on, and descend again, until they arrive at a deep crypt whose "walls had been lined with human remains, piled to the vault overhead." Jubilant until now in his pursuit, but now disbelieving, hysterical, Fortunato—man—cries out, as he faces his own destruction, "A very good joke, indeed—an excellent jest." Man's fate is death, not life, not the Amontillado he seeks with such joyful eagerness. Life is a jest, man's hope as illusory as the wine, his real nature surmounted

---

[5] In a review of the poems of H. B. Hirst in the *Broadway Journal*, July 12, 1845.

[6] *Poe: A Critical Study*, 182 (Cambridge, Mass., 1957), 182.

with cap and bells, his role no more real than that of the jester in carnival time. If all this seems so familiar, it is because so much in contemporary literature derives from a tradition which had its origin in Poe.

No less interesting as allegory and symbol than "The Cask of Amontillado" is "The Masque of the Red Death" (1842). Again the scene is a masquerade, this time a masked ball in a secluded, palatial abbey at which Prince Prospero and "a thousand hale and light-hearted friends" celebrate their six months' escape from the plague known as the Red Death. Poe described the revels as a voluptuous scene of unusual magnificence set in a suite of rooms whose description and the action within them Poe clearly intended to be associated with the seven ages of man. There were seven imperial apartments "so irregularly disposed that the vision embraced but little more than one at a time." Each provided "a sharp turn at every twenty or thirty yards, and at each turn a novel effect." Each room, beginning with the one "at the eastern extremity," contained ornaments and draperies to match the color of the stained glass in the Gothic windows. The seventh, the "western or black chamber," was draped in black but its windows were "a deep blood color," for a brazier of fire which projected its rays through the glass illumined the room with "a multitude of gaudy and fantastic appearances." In this western chamber stood an ebony clock whose pendulum "swung to and fro with a dull, heavy, monotonous clang," and while its chimes rang, "the giddiest grew pale, and the more aged and sedate passed their hands over their brows as if in confused reveries or meditation." It was the Prince's "own guiding tastes which had given character to the masqueraders."

There were delirious fancies such as the madman fashions. There was much of the beautiful, much of the wanton, much of the *bizarre,* something of the terrible, and not a little of that which might have excited disgust. To and fro in the seven chambers there stalked, in fact, a multitude of dreams.

In the densely crowded apartments "beat feverishly the heart of life," and "the revel went whirlingly on" until the ebony clock struck the midnight hour and the merriment yielded first to "disapprobation and surprise" and then to "terror, horror," as there appeared the figure attired as the Red Death, "tall and gaunt, and shrouded from head to foot in the habiliments of the grave." Prince Prospero rushed at the intruder with his dagger but "fell prostrate in death," and as the revellers seized the mummer, "whose tall figure stood erect and motionless within the shadow of the ebony clock," they gasped in horror to find "the grave-cerements and corpse-like mask . . . untenanted by any tangible form."

And one by one dropped the revellers in the blood-bedewed halls of their revel, and died each in the despairing posture of his fall. . . . And Darkness and Decay and the Red Death held illimitable dominion over all.

The story reduced to a summary, the symbols become obvious. The narrative elements disguise only vaguely the repeated formula of Death as the Conqueror Worm, the prevailing theme before *Eureka.* The symbols are many: the suite of seven rooms representative of life's periods, the first in the eastern end and the last in the west and its colors black and red; the ebony clock which strikes the hours of life and in whose shadow the mysterious mummer stands while the throng fall dead—as time and death assume a simultaneous significance; the description of the revels as a *danse macabre* of life; the symbolism of the mask itself, especially that of the Red Death as but one of Death's many forms. The Prince ironically bears the name of Shakespeare's hero, for he possesses none of his powers. This is no magic isle; nature will not be subdued, and it is death, not love, which conquers all. Here, as in so many of his poems and stories, Poe told the same story, but with a narrative skill and an imagination so great that the result is like a mask but behind which lurks the formula which was its inspiration.

# Conclusion

FOR THE POEM AND THE SHORT STORY Poe demanded a unity of effect to result from "no word written, of which the tendency, direct or indirect, is not to the one preestablished design." The word in literature is like the atom in the universe; as every atom relates to every other, so should every word in a poem or story relate to every other word for perfect rhythmical unity. Art must re-create the rhythmical operation of the universe, and so Poe repeated in his own way that art must imitate nature. In *Marginalia*, Poe defined art as the "reproduction of what the senses perceive in nature through the veil of the soul," and in the conclusion to "The Poetic Principle" (1850) he glorified in detail those elements in nature which inspire the artist to a realization of the "supernal Loveliness."

He recognizes the ambrosia which nourishes his soul, in the bright orbs that shine in Heaven—in the volutes of the flower—in the clustering of low shrubberies—in the waving of the grain-fields—in the slanting of tall, Eastern trees—in the blue distance of mountains—in the grouping of clouds—in the twinkling of half-hidden brooks—in the gleaming of silver rivers—in the repose of sequestered lakes—in the star-mirroring depths of lonely wells. He perceives it in the songs of birds—in the harp of Aeolus—in the sighing of the night-wind—in the repining voice of the forest—in the surf that complains to the shore—in the fresh breath of the woods—in the scent of the violet—in the voluptuous perfume of the hyacinth—in the suggestive odor that comes to him, at eventide, from far-distant, undiscovered islands, over dim oceans, illimitable and unexplored. He owns it in all noble thoughts—in all unworldly motives—in all holy impulses—in all chivalrous, generous, and self-sacrificing deeds. He feels it in the beauty of woman—in the grace of her step—in the lustre of her eye—in the melody of her voice—in her soft laughter—in her sigh—in the harmony of the rustling of her robes. He deeply feels it in her winning endearments—in her burning enthusiasms—in her gentle charities—in her meek and devotional endurances—but above all—ah, far above all—he kneels to it—he worships it in the faith, in the purity, in the strength, in the altogether divine majesty—of her *love*.

The artist's harmonious re-creation of these elements parallels the rhythmical creation of beauty observed in the universe itself.

Poe's principles of artistic creation became in effect the scientific principles of the universe as he recorded them in *Eureka*. Science is the art of God, and the artist strives to re-create the harmony which he observes in scientific unity. Poe's view of the analogy between artistic and divine creation has already been carefully observed by Carol Hopkins Maddison in her essay, "Poe's *Eureka*," and by Margaret Alterton in an earlier study, "The Origins of Poe's Critical Theory." The progression from "Poetic Principle" to *Eureka*, Poe himself foresaw in the first: "The struggle to apprehend the supernal Loveliness—this struggle, on the part of souls fittingly constituted—has given to the world all that which it (the world) has ever been enabled at once to understand and *to feel* as poetic." The artist's apprehen sion of the divine magic permits the world a glimpse of the glory possible only in the reunion between matter and origin. "And thus when by poetry . . . we find ourselves melted into tears . . . impatient sorrow at our inability to grasp *now*, wholly, here on earth, at once and for ever, those divine and rapturous joys, of which *through* the poem, or *through* the music, we attain to but brief and indeterminate glimpses."

Poe's work may reflect an abnormal psychology. It may even reflect, as D. H. Lawrence observed, "distintegration processes of his own Psyche." But more significantly, Poe's work is an illustration of an observation which to him was truth. Not his own disintegration but the disintegration of all reality was his theme. Poem after poem and story after story identify this interpretation, to which in *Eureka* he added the romantic conclusion that dissolution and death are phases of a process climaxed by the return of all diffused matter to its beginning. In what must have been his own copy of the first edition of *Eureka*, Poe recorded in his own hand at the end of his notes intended for a future edition this final notation:

> The pain of the consideration that we shall lose our individual identity, ceases at once when we reflect that the process, as above described, is, neither more nor less than that of the absorption, by each individual intelligence, of all other intelligences (that is, of the Universe) into its own. That God may be all in all, each must become God.[1]

Poe needed to believe in a purpose for all dissolution, and

[1] James A. Harrison (ed.), *Complete Works* of Edgar Allan Poe (New York, 1902), XVI, 336.

he found it finally in his theory of ultimate reunion between created matter and God. "The Raven" and "Ulalume" having expressed his rejection of a physical resurrection, the reunion between the particled and the unparticled became his substitute for heaven. After the earthly experience of sorrow and death, repeatedly recorded in verse and fiction, *Eureka* became Poe's vision of a life beyond the reality of matter, a scientific and metaphysical paradise, which, we know from his own testimony, Poe considered his final word.

# A Bibliography of Poe Criticism

This bibliography presumes to include all the books written about Poe, in whole or in part, since his death in 1849, and all the periodical essays published since 1925. The abbreviations used in the periodical references are those of the Modern Language Association.

## 1. BOOKS

Allen, Gay W. *American Prosody*. New York and Cincinnati, 1935.

Allen, Hervey. *Israfel: The Life and Times of Edgar Allan Poe*. New York, 1926.

———. Introduction to Modern Library Edition of *Complete Tales and Poems* of Edgar Allan Poe. New York, 1965.

———, and Thomas O. Mabbott. *Poe's Brothers*. New York, 1927.

Alterton, Margaret. *Origins of Poe's Critical Theory*. New York, 1965.

———, and Hardin Craig. *Edgar Allan Poe: Representative Selections*. Introduction, Bibliography, and Notes. New York, 1935, 1962; Gloucester, Mass., 1962.

Asselineau, Roger, ed. *Edgar Poe: Choix de Contes*. Parallcl

Text with Baudelaire Translation. Introduction. Paris, 1958.

Auden, W. H., ed. *Selected Prose and Poetry* of Edgar Allan Poe. Introduction. New York, 1942.

Baldwin, C. S. "Poe's Invention of the Short Story," in *American Short Stories*. New York, 1904.

Bandy, William. *The Influence and Reputation of Edgar Allan Poe in Europe.* Baltimore, 1962.

Basler, Roy P. *Sex, Symbolism, and Psychology in Literature*. New Brunswick, 1948.

Baudelaire, Charles. *Baudelaire on Poe*. Critical Papers trans. by Lois and Francis Hyslop, Jr., State College, Pa., 1962.

————. "Edgar Poe, sa vie et ses oeuvres," in *Histoires extraordinaires* par Edgar Poe. Paris, 1856; trans. by H. C. Curwin, London, 1872.

————. "Notes nouvelles sur Edgar Poe," in *Nouvelles histoires extraordinaires*. Paris, 1857.

Bayless, Joy. *Rufus Wilmot Griswold*. Nashville, 1943.

Belden, Henry M. "Observation and Imagination in Coleridge and Poe: A Contrast," *In Honor of the Ninetieth Birthday of Charles Frederick Johnson*. Hartford, Conn., 1928.

Bell, Landon C. *Poe and Chivers*. Columbus, Ohio, 1931.

Benét, Laura. *Young Edgar Allan Poe*. New York, 1941.

Benton, Joe. *In the Poe Circle*. New York, 1899.

Betz, L. P. "Edgar Poe in der französischen Litteratur," in *Studien zur vergleichenden Litteraturgeschichte der neuren Zeit*. Frankfurt, 1902.

Bewley, Edmund. *The Origins and Early History of the Family of Poe*. Dublin, 1906.

Bezanson, Walter E. "The Troubled Sleep of Arthur Gordon Pym," in Rudolf Kirk and C. F. Main (eds.), *Essays in Literary History*. New Brunswick, N.J., 1960.

Biedy, H. A. *Mysteries of Poe's Raven*. New York, 1936.

Bittner, William R. *Poe: A Biography*. Boston, 1962.

Blöcker, Günter, ed. *Meistererzählungen*. Bremen, 1960.

Bonaparte, Marie. *Life and Works of Edgar Allan Poe*. Trans. by John Rodker. London, 1949.

Bondurant, Agnes. *Poe's Richmond*. Richmond, 1942.

Booth, B. A., and C. E. Jones. *Concordance of the Poetical Works of Edgar Allan Poe*. Baltimore, 1941; Magnolia, Mass., 1967.

Braddy, Haldeen. *Glorious Incense: The Fulfillment of Edgar Allan Poe*. Washington, 1953; Port Washington, N.Y., 1968.

Bragg, C. W., comp. *Material by and about Edgar Allan Poe in the Library of Columbia University*. New York, 1909.

Brenner, Rica. *Twelve American Poets before 1900*. New York, 1933.

Brooks, Cleanth, and Robert Penn Warren. *Understanding Fiction*. New York, 1943.

Broussard, Louis. *The Measure of Poe*. Norman, Okla., 1969.

Brownell, W. C. *American Prose Masters*. New York, 1909, 1935, 1963.

Buchholz, H. E., ed. *Edgar Allan Poe: A Centenary Tribute*. Baltimore, 1910.

Buranelli, Vincent. *Edgar Allan Poe*. New York, 1961.

Cain, Henry E. *James Clarence Mangan and the Poe-Mangan Question*. Washington, 1929.

Cambiaire, C. P. *The Influence of Edgar Allan Poe in France*. New York, 1927.

Campbell, Killis. *The Mind of Poe and Other Studies.* New York, 1933, 1962.

———. Biographical Note to the Facsimile Edition of the 1831 Edition of *Poems* of Edgar Allan Poe. New York, 1936.

———, ed. *The Poems of Edgar Allan Poe.* Introduction and Notes. New York, 1917, 1962.

———. *Poe's Tales.* Introduction. New York, 1927.

Canby, Henry S. *The Short Story in English.* New York, 1909.

Carlson, Eric W. *Introduction to Poe: A Thematic Reader.* Glenview, Ill., 1967.

———, ed. *The Recognition of Edgar Allan Poe.* East Lansing, Mich., 1966.

Charvat, William. "Poe: Journalism and the Theory of Poetry," in Richard Ludwig (ed.), *Aspects of American Poetry.* Columbus, Ohio, 1962.

Chase, L. N. *Poe and His Poetry.* London, 1913.

Chiari, Joseph. *Symbolisme from Poe to Mallarmé.* Foreword by T. S. Eliot. London, 1956; New York, 1957.

Chivers, Thomas Holley. *Chivers' Life of Poe.* Ed. with an Introduction by Richard Davis. New York, 1952.

Cobb, Palmer. *The Influence of E. T. A. Hoffman on the Tales of Edgar Allan Poe.* Chapel Hill, 1908.

Cody, Sherwin. *Poe: Man, Poet, and Creative Thinker.* New York, 1924.

Colling, Alfred. *Edgar Poe.* Paris, 1952.

Conner, F. W. *Cosmic Optimism: A Study of the Interpretation of Evolution by American Poets from Emerson to Robinson.* Gainesville, Fla., 1949.

Cooke, John Esten. *Poe as a Literary Critic.* Baltimore, 1946.

Cooper, L. U. *The Young Edgar Allan Poe.* Toronto, 1964.

Dameron, J. L. *Edgar Allan Poe: A Checklist of Criticism, 1942–1960.* Charlottesville, 1966.

————. *An Index to Poe's Critical Vocabulary.* Hartford, Conn., 1966.

Damon, S. F. *Thomas Holley Chivers, Friend of Poe.* New York, 1930.

Davidson, Edward. *Poe: A Critical Study.* Cambridge, Mass., 1957.

————, ed. *Selected Writings of Edgar Allan Poe.* Introduction and Notes. Boston, 1956.

DeMille, George E. *Literary Criticism in America.* New York, 1931.

Didier, Eugene. *Life and Poems of Edgar A. Poe.* Introductory Letter by Sarah Helen Whitman. New York, 1879.

————. *The Poe Cult and Other Papers.* New York, 1909.

Dillon, John. *Edgar Allan Poe: His Genius and His Character.* New York, 1911.

Douglas-Lithgow, R. A. *Individuality of Edgar Allan Poe.* Boston, 1911.

Dow, Dorothy. *Dark Glory.* New York, 1931.

Durick, Jeremiah K. "The Incorporate Silence and the Heart Divine," in Harold C. Gardiner (ed.), *American Classics Reconsidered.* New York, 1958.

Eliot, T. S. *From Poe to Valéry.* New York, 1948.

————. *Notes Towards a Definition of Culture.* New York, 1949.

————. *To Criticize the Critic.* London, 1965.

Empson, William. *Some Versions of the Pastoral.* London, 1935.

Englekirk, John. *Edgar Allan Poe in Hispanic Literature.* New York, 1934.

Evans, H. R. *Edgar Allan Poe and Baron von Kempelen's Chess-Playing Automaton*. Washington, D.C., 1939.

Evans, May G. *Music and Edgar Allan Poe: A Biographical Study*. Baltimore, 1939.

Eveleth, G. W. *Letters to Edgar Allan Poe*. New York, 1922.

Ewers, Hanns H. *Edgar Allan Poe*. New York, 1916.

Fagin, Nathan B. *The Histrionic Mr. Poe*. Baltimore, 1949.

Feidelson, Charles, Jr. *Symbolism and American Literature*. Chicago, 1953.

Ferguson, John D. *American Literature in Spain*. New York, 1913.

Foerster, Norman. *American Criticism: A Study in Literary Theory from Poe to the Present*. Boston, 1928; New York, 1962.

Forrest, William. *Biblical Allusions in Poe*. New York, 1928.

French, John C., ed. *Poe in Foreign Lands and Tongues*. Baltimore, 1941.

Fruit, John P. *The Mind and Art of Poe's Poetry*. New York, 1899.

Gates, L. E. *Studies and Appreciations*. New York, 1900.

Gill, William F. *Life of Edgar Allan Poe*. New York, 1877.

Gohdes, Clarence. *American Literature in Nineteenth-Century England*. New York, 1944.

Gordon, John W. *Edgar Allan Poe: An Exhibition on the Centenary of His Death*. A Catalogue of First Editions, Manuscripts, Autograph Letters from the Berg Collection, New York Public Library. New York, 1949.

Graham, Kenneth. Introduction to *Selected Tales* of Edgar Allan Poe. London, 1967.

Grava, Arnolds. *L'aspect métaphysique du mal dans l'oeuvre littéraire de Charles Baudelaire et d'Edgar Allan Poe.* Univ of Neb Studies, n.s., No. 15. Lincoln, Neb., 1956.

Green, A. W. "The Weekly Magazines and Poe," in *English Studies in Honor of James Southall Wilson.* Charlottesville, 1951.

Griswold, Rufus W., ed. *Works* of Edgar Allen Poe. 4 vols. Memoir in Vol. III. New York, 1850–56.

Harrison, James A. *Life and Letters* of Edgar Allan Poe. New York, 1903.

———. *New Glimpses of Poe.* New York, 1901.

———, ed. *Complete Works* of Edgar Allan Poe. 17 vols. New York, 1902.

———, ed. *The Last Letters of Edgar Allan Poe to Sarah Helen Whitman.* New York and London, 1909.

Hatvary, George E., and Thomas O. Mabbott. A Photographic Facsimile Edition of Poe's *Prose Romances: Murders in the Rue Morgue and The Man That Was Used Up.* Introduction by George E. Hatvary. New York, 1968.

Hazelton, G. C. *Raven: Love Story of Edgar Allan Poe.* New York, 1909.

Heartman, Charles F., and James R. Canny. A *Bibliography of First Printings of the Writings of Edgar Allan Poe.* Hattiesburg, Miss., 1940; rev. ed., 1943.

———, and Kenneth Rede. *Census of First Editions and Source Materials by Edgar Allan Poe in American Collections.* Metuchen, N.J., 1932.

———, and Kenneth Rede. *Edgar Allan Poe's Contributions to Annuals and Periodicals.* Metuchen, N.J., 1932.

Hewitt, John Hill. *Recollections of Poe.* Atlanta, 1949.

Higginson, Thomas Wentworth. *Short Studies in American Authors.* Boston, 1879.

Hough, Robert L. *Literary Criticism of Edgar Allan Poe.* Lincoln, Neb., 1965.

Hubbell, Jay B. "Poe," in Floyd Stovall (ed.), *Eight American Authors.* New York, 1956.

———. *The South in American Literature.* Durham, N.C., 1954.

Hudson, Ruth. "Poe Recognizes 'Ligeia' as His Masterpiece," in *English Studies in Honor of James Southall Wilson.* Charlottesville, 1951.

Hutton, R. H. *Criticisms on Contemporary Thought and Thinkers.* London, 1900.

Huxley, Aldous. *Vulgarity in Literature.* London, 1930.

*Index to Early American Periodical Literature, 1728–1870.* Part 2, Edgar Allan Poe. Introduction by Thomas O. Mabbott. New York, 1941.

Ingram, John H. *Edgar Allan Poe: His Life, Letters, and Opinions.* London, 1880.

———. *The Raven . . . with Literary and Historical Commentary.* London, 1885.

Jackowska, S. d'O. *La Rehabilitation de Edgar Poe et ses plus beaux poemes en vers français.* New York, 1933.

Jackson, David K. *Poe and the Southern Literary Messenger.* Richmond, 1934.

———. *The Contributors and Contributions to the Southern Literary Messenger.* Charlottesville, 1935.

Jacobs, Robert D. "Poe in Richmond: The Double Image," in Richard Meeker (ed.), *The Dilemma of the Southern Writer.* Farmville, Va., 1961.

James, Henry. "Baudelaire," in *French Poets and Novelists.* New York, 1964.

———. *Hawthorne.* London, 1879; New York, 1880.

Joyce, John A. *Edgar Allan Poe.* New York, 1901.

Keily, Jarvis. *Edgar Allan Poe: A Probe.* New York, 1927.

Kent, Charles W. "Poe the Poet," Introduction to Vol. VII of J. A. Harrison (ed.), *Complete Works* of Edgar Allan Poe. New York, 1902.

——, and J. S. Patton, eds. *The Book of the Poe Centenary*. A Record of Exercises at the University of Virginia, January 16–19, 1909. Charlottesville, 1909.

Krutch, Joseph Wood. *Edgar Allan Poe; A Study in Genius*. New York, 1926, 1965.

Kühnelt, H. H. *Die Bedeutung von Edgar Allan Poe für die englische Literatur*. Innsbruck, 1949.

Lang, Andrew. *Letters to Dead Authors*. London, 1886.

Lauvrière, Emile. *Edgar Poe, sa vie et son oeuvre, étude de psychologie pathologique*. Paris, 1904.

——. *The Strange Life and Strange Loves of Edgar Allan Poe*. Trans. by E. G. Rich. Philadelphia, 1935.

Lawrence, D. H. *Studies in Classic American Literature*. New York, 1923.

Leigh, Oliver. *Edgar Allan Poe*. A Study of the Portraits of Poe. Chicago, 1906.

——. *Edgar Allan Poe: The Man, The Master, The Martyr*. Chicago, 1906.

Lemonnier, Leon. *Edgar Poe et la Critique française de 1845 à 1875*. Paris, 1928.

——. *Edgar Poe et les poètes français*. Paris, 1932.

——. *Les Traducteurs d'Edgar Poe en France de 1845 à 1875*. Paris, 1928.

Lenhart, Charmenz S. *Musical Influence on American Poetry*. Athens, Ga., 1956.

Levin, Harry. *The Power of Blackness*. New York, 1958.

Lindsay, Philip. *The Haunted Man; A Portrait of Edgar Allan Poe*. London, 1953.

Lloyd, John A. *The Murder of Edgar Allan Poe*. London, 1931.

Lubbers, Klaus. *Die Todesszene und ihre Funktion im Kurzgeschichtenwerk von Edgar Allan Poe*. Munich, 1961.

Mabbott, Thomas Olive. Biographical Note to the Facsimile Edition of the 1829 edition of *Al Aaraaf*. New York, 1933.

———. Preface, Introduction, and Comments to Poe's *Doings of Gotham*. Poe's Contributions to the *Columbia Spy*. Collected by Jacob E. Spannuth. Pottsville, Pa., 1929.

———. Introduction to the Facsimile Edition of the Lorimer Graham copy of the 1845 Edition of *The Raven and Other Poems*. New York, 1942.

———. Introduction to the Facsimile Edition of the 1827 Edition of *Tamerlane and Other Poems*. New York, 1941.

———. *Politian*; An Unfinished Tragedy by Edgar Allan Poe; Including Unpublished Scenes from the Manuscript in the Pierpont Morgan Library. Notes and Commentary. Richmond, 1916.

Macy, John A. *Edgar Allan Poe*. Boston, 1907.

Markham, Edwin. "Poe," in John Macy (ed.), *American Writers on American Literature*. New York, 1931.

Marks, Jeannette A. *Genius and Disaster; Studies in Drugs and Genius*. New York, 1925.

Matthews, Brander. *An Introduction to the Study of American Literature*. New York, 1896.

———. "Poe and the Detective Story," in *Inquiries and Opinions*. New York, 1907.

Mauclair, Camille. *Le Genie d'Edgar Poe*. Paris, 1925.

Messac, Regis. *Influences françaises dans l'oeuvre d'Edgar Poe*. Paris, 1929.

Miller, J. C. *John Henry Ingram's Poe Collection at the University of Virginia*. Charlottesville, 1960.

Miller, Perry. *The Raven and the Whale*. New York, 1956.

Moran, John J. *A Defense of Edgar Allan Poe*. Washington, 1885.

More, Paul Elmer. "The Origins of Hawthorne and Poe," in *Shelburne Essays*. First series. New York, 1904.

Morton, Maxwell. *Builder of the Beautiful; Some Unsuspected Aspects of Poe*. Boston, 1928.

Moses, Montrose J. *The Literature of the South*. New York, 1910.

Moss, Sidney. *Poe's Literary Battles*. Durham, N.C., 1963.

Murch, A. E. *The Development of the Detective Novel*. London, 1958.

Nakamura, Junichi. *Edgar Allan Poe's Relations with New England*. Tokyo, 1957.

Nichols, Mary G. *Reminiscences of Edgar Allan Poe*. New York, 1931.

Ober, Warren U., and others, ed. *The Enigma of Poe*. Boston, 1960.

Olivero, Frederico. *Edgar Poe*. Trans. by Dante Milani. Torino, 1939.

Osgoode, Joseph A. "Poe the Artist," in *Tell It in Gath*. Sewanee, Tenn., 1918.

Ostrom, John Ward, ed. *The Letters* of Edgar Allan Poe. Cambridge, Mass., 1948; Brooklyn, N.Y., 1966.

———, comp. *Check List of Letters to and from Poe*. Charlottesville, 1941.

Parks, E. W. *Edgar Allan Poe as Literary Critic*. Athens, Ga., 1964.

Parrington, Vernon L. *Main Currents in American Thought*. Vol. II. New York, 1927.

Partridge, H. M., and D. C. Partridge. *The Most Remarkable Echo in the World*. Hastings-on-Hudson, N.Y., 1933.

Pattee, F. L. *The Development of the American Short Story.* New York, 1923.

Perry, Marvin B. "Keats and Poe," in *English Studies in Honor of James Southall Wilson.* Charlottesville, 1951.

Phillips, Mary E. *Edgar Allan Poe, the Man.* Chicago, 1926.

Pichois, Claude, ed. *Adventures d'Arthur Gordon Pym . . .* avec la conclusion imagineé par Jules Verne dans *Le Spinx des Glaces.* Paris, 1960.

Poe, Elizabeth and Vylla Wilson. *Edgar Allen Poe, a High Priest of the Beautiful.* A Biographical Essay. Washington, 1930.

Poe, William Henry Leonard. *Poe's Brother: The Poems of William Henry Leonard Poe.* Preface, Introduction, and Comment by Hervey Allen and Thomas O. Mabbott. New York, 1926.

Pollin, B. R. *Dictionary of Names and Titles in Poe's Collected Works.* New York, 1968.

Pope-Hennessy, Una. *Edgar Allan Poe: A Critical Biography.* London, 1934.

Porges, Irwin. *Edgar Allan Poe.* Philadelphia, 1963.

Quinn, Arthur Hobson. *Edgar Allan Poe; A Critical Biography.* New York, 1941.

———. Introduction and Explanatory Notes to *Complete Poems and Stories* of Edgar Allan Poe. New York, 1946.

———, and Richard H. Hart, eds. *Letters and Documents in the Enoch Pratt Free Library.* New York, 1941.

Quinn, Patrick. *The French Face of Edgar Poe.* Carbondale, Ill., 1957.

Randall, David A. *The J. K. Lilly Collection of Edgar Allan Poe; An Account of Its Formation.* Bloomington, Ind., 1964.

Rans, Geoffrey. *Edgar Allan Poe.* Edinburgh, 1965.

Ransome, Arthur. *Edgar Allan Poe; A Critical Study*. London, 1910.

Regan, Robert, ed. *Poe; A Collection of Critical Essays*. Englewood Cliffs, N.J., 1967.

Rein, David. *Edgar Allan Poe: The Inner Pattern*. New York, 1960.

Rice, Sara S., ed. *Edgar Allan Poe; A Memorial Volume*. Baltimore, 1877.

Richardson, Charles F. *American Literature, 1607–1885*. Vol. II. New York, 1889.

Robertson, John W. *Bibliography of the Writings of Edgar A. Poe*. San Francisco, 1934.

———. *Edgar Allan Poe; A Psychopathic Study*. San Francisco, 1921.

Rogers, David M. *The Major Poems and Tales of Edgar Allan Poe*. New York, 1966.

Schuhmann, Kuno. *Die Erzahlende Prosa Edgar Allan Poe: Ein Beitrag zu einer Gattungsgeschichte der "short story."* Heidelberg, 1958.

Schulte, Amanda Pogue. *Facts about Poe: Portraits and Daguerreotypes of Edgar Allan Poe*. With a Sketch of the Life of Poe by James Southall Wilson. Charlottesville, 1926.

Seylaz, Louis. *Edgar Poe et les premiers symbolistes français*. Lausanne, 1923.

Shanks, Edward. *Edgar Allan Poe*. London, 1937.

Simpson, Lewis P. " 'Touching "The Stylus" ' ": Notes on Poe's Vision of Literary Order," in Waldo McNeir and Lee Levy (eds.), *Studies in American Literature*. Baton Rouge, La., 1960.

Slater, Montagu, ed. *Centenary Poe*. New York, 1950.

Smith, Clarence Alphonso. *Edgar Allan Poe: How To Know Him*. Indianapolis, 1921.

Snell, George. *The Shapers of American Fiction, 1798–1947.* New York, 1947, 1961.

Spiller, Robert E. "The American Literary Dilemma and Edgar Allan Poe," in Carl Bode (ed.), *The Great Experiment in American Literature.* New York, 1961.

Stanard, Mary N. *The Dreamer; A Romantic Rendering of the Life-Story of Edgar Allan Poe.* Richmond, 1909.

———. Introductory Essay and Commentary in *Letters Till Now Unpublished, in the Valentine Museum, Richmond,* by Edgar Allan Poe. Philadelphia, 1925.

Stedman, Edmund Clarence. *Edgar Allan Poe.* Boston, 1881.

———. *Poets and Poetry of America.* Boston, 1898.

———, and George Woodberry, eds. *Works* of Edgar Allan Poe. 10 vols. Chicago, 1894–95.

Stern, Philip Van Doren, ed. The Viking Portable Editions of *Edgar Allan Poe.* Introduction. New York, 1945.

Stewart, Robert A. *Case of Edgar Allan Poe.* A Pathological Study Based on the Investigations of Lauvière. Richmond, 1910.

Stoddard, Richard H. "Memoir," in *Poems* by Edgar Allan Poe. New York, 1875.

———. *Recollections, Personal and Literary.* New York, 1903.

———. *Works* of Edgar Allan Poe. Introduction and Memoir. 5 vols. New York, 1884.

Stovall, Floyd. Introduction to the *Poems of Edgar Allan Poe.* Charlottesville, 1965.

———, ed. *Eight American Authors; A Review of Research and Criticism.* New York, 1956.

———, ed. *The Poems of Edgar Allan Poe.* Introduction, Variant Readings, Textual Notes. Charlottesville, 1965.

Strickland, William W. *The Great Divide*. Part I: The Numerical Element in Edgar Allan Poe's Twelve Great Poems. New York, 1931.

Strong, Augustus. *American Poets and Their Theology*. Philadelphia, 1916.

Tate, Allen. *The Forlorn Demon*. Chicago, 1953.

Taupin, René. *L'Influence du Symbolisme français sur la poésie américaine*. Paris, 1929.

Thompson, John R. *The Genius and Character of Edgar Allan Poe*. Privately printed, 1929.

Ticknor, Caroline. *Poe's Helen*. New York, 1916.

Trent, William P. "The Centenary of Poe," in *Longfellow and Other Essays*. New York, 1910.

Trent, William P., and others. *Edgar Allan Poe; A Centenary Tribute*. Baltimore, 1910.

University of Virginia Library. *John Henry Ingram's Poe Collection at the University of Virginia*. Charlottesville, 1960.

Valéry, Paul. *Variety; Second Series*. Trans. by William Bradley. New York, 1938.

Varner, John G. Introduction to *Edgar Allan Poe and the Philadelphia Saturday Courier*. Facsimile Reproductions of the First Texts of Poe's Earliest Tales. Charlottesville, 1933.

Wachtler, P. *Edgar Allan Poe und die deutsche Romantik*. Leipzig, 1911.

Wagenknecht, Edward. *Edgar Allan Poe; The Man Behind the Legend*. New York, 1963.

Wallace, Alfred R. *Edgar Allan Poe*; A Series of Seventeen Letters Concerning Poe's Scientific Erudition in *Eureka* and His Authorship of "Leonainie." New York, 1930.

Walsh, J. E. *Poe the Detective*. New Brunswick, N. J., 1968.

Weiss, Susan A. *The Home Life of Poe.* New York, 1907.

Wells, Gabriel. *Edgar Allan Poe as a Mystic.* Metuchen, N.J., 1934.

Whitman, Sarah Helen. *Edgar Allan Poe and His Critics.* New York, 1860; New Brunswick, 1949.

———. *Was Poe Immoral?* Girard, Kansas, 1923(?).

Whitman, Walt. *Specimen Days.* Vol. I of *Complete Prose Works.* New York and London, 1902.

Whitty, J. H. "Memoir," in the *Complete Poems of Edgar Allan Poe.* Boston, 1917.

Williams, W. C. *In the American Grain.* New York, 1925.

Wilmer, Lambert A. *Merlin, Baltimore, 1827; Together with Recollections of Edgar Allan Poe.* Ed. with an Introduction by Thomas O. Mabbott. New York, 1941.

Wilson, Edmund. "Poe at Home and Abroad," in *A Literary Chronicle, 1920–1950.* Garden City, N.Y., 1956.

Wilson, James S., ed. *Letters to George W. Eveleth* by Edgar Allan Poe. Charlottesville, 1924.

Winters, Yvor. "Edgar Allan Poe: A Crisis in the History of American Obscurantism," in *Maule's Curse.* Norfolk, Conn., 1938.

Winwar, Frances. *The Haunted Palace; A Life of Edgar Allan Poe.* New York, 1959.

Woodberry, George. *Edgar Allan Poe.* American Men of Letters. Boston, 1885.

———. *The Life of Edgar Allan Poe, Personal and Literary, with His Chief Correspondence with Men of Letters.* Boston, 1909; New York, 1965.

Wyllie, John C. "A List of the Texts of Poe's Tales," in *Humanistic Studies in Honor of John Calvin Metcalf.* Charlottesville, 1941.

## 2. PERIODICAL ESSAYS SINCE 1925

Abel, Darrel. "Coleridge's 'Life-in-Death' and Poe's 'Death-in-Life,'" *N & Q*, n.s., II (1955), 218–20.

——. "Edgar Poe: A Centennial Estimate," *UKCR*, XVI (1949), 77–96.

——. "A Key to the House of Usher," *UTQ*, XVIII (1949), 176–85.

Acosta, Leonardo. "Edgar Allan Poe," *Nueva Revista Cubano*, I (1959), 50–65.

Adams, Percy G. "Poe, Critic of Voltaire," *MLN*, LVII (1942), 273–75.

Adkins, Nelson F. " 'Chapter on American Cribbage': Poe and Plagiarism," *PBSA*, XLII (1948), 169–210.

——. "Poe's Borrowings," *N & Q*, CLXVII (1934), 67–68.

——. "Poe's 'Ulalume,' " *N & Q*, CLXIV (1933), 30–31.

Adler, Jacob. "Are There Flaws in 'The Cask of Amontillado'?" *N & Q*, CXCIX (1954), 32–34.

Alderman, E. A. "Edgar Allan Poe and the University of Virginia," *VQR*, I (1925), 78–84.

Alexander, Jean A. "Affidavits of Genius: French Essays on Poe from Forgues to Valéry," *DA*, XXII, 866.

Allan, Carlisle. "Cadet Edgar Allan Poe, U.S.A." *Am Mer*, XXIX (1933), 446–55.

Allen, James L., Jr. "Stanza Pattern in the Poetry of Poe," *TSL*, XII (1967), 111–20.

Allen, Mozelle S. "Poe's Debt to Voltaire," *UTSE*, XV (1935), 63–75.

Almy, Robert F. "J. N. Reynolds: A Brief Biography with Reference to Poe and Symmes," *Colophon*, n.s., II (1937), 217–21.

Alterton, Margaret. "An Additional Source for Poe's 'The Pit and the Pendulum,'" *MLN*, XLVIII (1933), 349–56.

———. "An Additional Source of Poe's Critical Theory," *Univ Iowa Stud*, II (1926).

———. "Origins of Poe's Critical Theory," *Univ of Iowa Humanistic Studies*, Vol. II, No. 3, 1925.

Amacher, Richard. "Poe's 'The City in the Sea,'" *Expl*, XIX (1961), Item 60.

Anderson, David. "A Comparison of the Poetic Theories of Emerson and Poe," *Person*, XLI (1960), 471–83.

Archibald, R. C. "Music and Edgar Allan Poe," *N & Q*, CLXXIX (1940), 170–71.

Arndt, K. J. "Poe's *Politian* and Goethe's *Mignon*," *MLN*, XLIX (1934), 101–104.

Arnold, John. "Poe's 'Lionizing': The Wound and the Bawdry," *L & P*, XVII (No. 1, 1967), 52–54.

Astrov, Vladimir. "Dostoievsky on Edgar Allan Poe," *AL*, XIV (1942), 70–74.

Babler, F. O. "Czech Translations of Poe's 'Raven,'" *N & Q*, CXCII (1947), 235.

———. "German Translations of Poe's 'Raven,'" *N & Q*, CLXXIV (1938), 9–10.

Bailey, J. O. "The Geography of Poe's 'Dreamland' and 'Ulalume,'" *SP*, XLV (1948), 512–23.

———. "Poe's 'Palestine,'" *AL*, XIII (1941), 44–58.

———. "Poe's 'Stonehenge,'" *SP*, XXXVIII (1941), 645–51.

———. "Sources of Poe's *Arthur Gordon Pym*, 'Hans Ffaal' and Other Pieces," *PMLA*, LVII (1942), 513–35.

———. "What Happens in 'The Fall of the House of Usher'?" *AL*, XXXV (1963–64), 445–66.

Bandy, W. T. "Baudelaire and Poe," *TQ*, I, Supplement (Feb., 1958), 28–35.

——. "An Imaginary Translation of Poe," *RLC*, XXXIII (1959), 87–90.

——. "New Light on a Source of Poe's 'A Descent into the Maelstrom,'" *AL*, XXIV (1953), 534–37.

——. "New Light on Baudelaire and Poe," *YFS*, No. 10 (1953), 65–69.

——. "Poe's Secret Translator: Amédée Pichot," *MLN*, LXXIX (1964), 277–80.

——. "Poe's Solution of 'The Frailey Land Office Cipher,'" *PMLA*, LXVIII (1953), 1240–41.

——. "A Source of Poe's 'The Premature Burial,'" *AL*, XIX (1947), 167–68.

——. "Were the Russians the First To Translate Poe?" *AL*, XXXI (1960), 479–80.

——. "Who Was Monsieur Dupin?" *PMLA*, LXXIX (1964), 509–10.

Basic, Sonja. "Edgar Allan Poe in Serbian and Croatian Literature," *Studia Romanica et Anglica Zagrebiensia*, Nos. 21–22, 305–19.

Baskett, S. A. "A Damsel with a Dulcimer: An Interpretation of Poe's 'Eleonora,'" *MLN*, LXXIII (1958), 332–38.

Basler, Roy P. "Byronism in Poe's 'To One in Paradise,'" *AL*, IX (1937), 232–36.

——. "The Interpretation of 'Ligeia,'" *CE*, V (1944), 363–72.

——. "Poe's 'City in the Sea,'" *Expl*, IV (1946), 30.

——. "Poe's 'The Valley of Unrest,'" *Expl*, V (1946), 25.

——. "Poe's 'Ulalume,'" *Expl*, II (1944), Item 49.

Baum, Paul. "Poe's 'To Helen,'" *MLN*, LXIV (1949), 289–97.

Bayliss, Joy. "Another Rufus W. Griswold as a Critic of Poe," *AL*, VI (1934), 69–72.

Baym, Nina. "The Function of Poe's Pictorialism," *SAQ*, LXV (1966), 46–54.

Beebe, Maurice. "The Fall of the House of Pyncheon," *NCF*, XI (1956), 1–17.

———. "The Universe of Roderick Usher," *Person*, XXXVII (1960), 147–60.

Belden, H. M. "Poe's 'The City in the Sea' and Dante's City of Dis," *AL*, VII (1935), 332–34.

Belgion, Montgomery. "The Mystery of Poe's Poetry," *EIC*, I (1951), 51–66.

Benson, A. B. "Scandinavian References in the Works of Poe," *JEGP*, XL (1941), 73–90.

Benton, Richard P. "Current Bibliography on Edgar Allan Poe," *ESQ*, XLVII, 84–87.

———. "Is Poe's 'The Assignation" a Hoax?" *NCF*, XVIII (1963), 193–97.

———. "The Works of N. P. Willis as a Catalyst of Poe's Criticism," *AL*, XXXIX, 315–24.

Bianchi, Ruggero. "Corollari di una Poetica del' l'effetto: I Marginalia di E. A. Poe," *RdE* (U. di Padova), XI (1966), 408–22.

Bierly, Charles H. "*Eureka* and the Drama of the Self: A Study of the Relationship Between Poe's Cosmology and His Fiction," *DA*, XVIII, 228–29.

Bignami, Marialuisa. "Edgar Allen Poe di fronte alla natura," *SA* (Roma), XI (1965), 105–15.

Binns, Elizabeth. "Daniel Bryan: Poe's Poet of the 'Good Old Goldsmith School,'" *WMQ*, Ser 2, XXIII (1943), 465–73.

Birss, J. H. "Poe in Fordham: A Reminiscence," *N & Q*, CLXXIII (1937), 440.

Bittner, William. "Poe and the 'Invisible Demon,' " *GaR*, XVII (1963), 134–38.

Blair, Walter. "Poe's Conception of Incident and Tone in the Tale," *MP*, XLI (1944), 228–40.

Blanch, Robert V. "The Background of Poe's 'Gold Bug,' " *English Record*, XVI, iv, 44–48.

———. "Poe's Imagery: An Undercurrent of Childhood Fears," *Furman Stud*, XIV, iv, 19–25.

Bledsoe, T. F. "On Poe's 'Valley of Unrest,' " *MLN*, LXI, (1946), 91–92.

Bohner, Charles. "The Poe-Kennedy Friendship," *PMHB*, LXXXII (1958), 220–22.

Boll, Ernest. "The Manuscript of 'The Murders of the Rue Morgue' and Poe's Revisions," *MP*, XL (1943), 302–15.

Bonaparte, Marie. "The Black Cat," *PR*, XVII (1950), 834–60.

Booth, Bradford A. "The Identity of Annabel Lee," *CE*, VII (1945), 17–19.

Boynton, Percy H. "Poe and Journalism," *EJ*, XXI (1932), 345–51.

Braddy, Haldeen. "Poe's Flight from Reality," *TSLL*, I (1959), 394–400.

Bradley, Sculley. "Poe on the New York Stage in 1855," *AL*, IX (1937), 353–54.

Brigham, C. S. "Edgar Allan Poe's Contributions to *Alexander's Weekly Messenger*," *PAAS*, LII (1942), 45–125.

Broderick, John. "Poe's Revisions of 'Lenore,' " *AL*, XXXV (1963–64), 504–10.

Burch, Francis F. "Clement Mansfield Ingleby on Poe's 'The Raven': An Unpublished British Criticism," *AL*, XXXV (1963), 81–83.

Burke, Kenneth. "The Principle of Composition," *Poetry*, XCIX (Oct, 1961), 46–53.

Cambiaire, C. P. "The Influence of Edgar Allan Poe in France," *RR*, XVII (1926), 319–37.

Cameron, Kenneth. Poe's 'Bells' and Schiller's 'Das Lied von der Glocke,' " *ESQ*, No. 19 (1960), 37.

———. "Poe's 'The Bells'—A Reply to Schiller and Romberg?" *ESQ*, No. 38 (1965), 2.

Campbell, Killis. "A Bit of Chiversian Mystification," *UTSE*, X (1930), 152–54.

———. "Marginalia on Longfellow, Lowell, and Poe," *MLN*, XLII (1927), 516–21.

———. "Poe's Knowledge of the Bible," *SP*, XXVII (1930), 546–51.

———. "Poe's Reading," *UTSE*, V (1925), 166–96.

———. "Poe's Reading: Addenda and Corrigenda," *UTSE*, VII (1927), 175–80.

———. "Poe's Treatment of the Negro and of Negro Dialect," *UTSE*, XVI (1936), 107–14.

———. "Three Notes on Poe," *AL*, IV (1933), 385–88.

———. "Who Was 'Outis'?" *UTSE*, VIII (1928), 107–109.

Caputi, Anthony. "The Refrain in Poe's Poetry," *AL*, XXV (1953), 169–78.

Cargill, Oscar. "A New Source for 'The Raven,' " *AL*, VIII (1936), 291–94.

Carley, C. V. "A Source for Poe's 'Oblong Box,' " *AL*, XXIX (1957), 310–12.

Carlson, Eric T. "Charles Poyen Brings Mesmerism to America," *Jour Hist Med*, XV (1960), 121–32.

———. "Poe's 'Eldorado,' " *MLN*, LXXVI (1961), 232–33.

———. "Poe's 'Ulalume,' 6–9," *Expl*, XI (1953), Item 56.

———. "Symbol and Sense in Poe's 'Ulalume,' " *AL*, XXXV (1963–64), 22–37.

Carson, David. "Ortolans and Geese: The Origin of Poe's *Duc de L'Omelette*," *CLAJ*, VIII (1965), 277–83.

Carter, Boyd. "Poe's Debt to Charles Brockden Brown," *PrS*, XXVII (1953), 190–96.

Cary, Richard. " 'The Masque of the Red Death' Again," *NCF*, XVII (1962), 76–78.

———. "Poe and the Great Debate," *TSLL*, III (1961), 223–33.

———. "Poe and the Literary Ladies," *TSLL*, IX (1967), 91–101.

Casale, Ottavio M. "Edgar Allan Poe and Transcendentalism: Conflict and Affinity," *DA*, XXVI, 6693.

Cauthen, I. B., Jr. "Lowell on Poe: An Unpublished Comment," *AL*, XXIV (1952), 230–32.

———. "Poe's 'Alone': Its Background, Source, and Manuscript," *SB*, III (1950), 284–91.

Cecil, L. M. "Poe's 'Arabesque,' " *CL*, XVIII (1966), 55–70.

———. "Poe's Tsalal and the Virginia Springs," *NCF*, XIX (1965), 398–402.

———. "The Two Narratives of Arthur Gordon Pym," *TSLL*, V (1963), 232–41.

Chari, V. K. "Poe and Whitman's Short-Poem Style," *WWR*, XIII (1967), 95–97.

Chase, Lewis. "A New Poe Letter," *AL*, VI (1934), 66–69.

Cherry, Fannye N. "The Source of Poe's 'Three Sundays in a Week,' " *AL*, II (1930), 232–35.

Chinol, Elio. "Poe's Essays on Poetry (1946)," *SR*, LXVIII (1960), 390–97.

Clark, David L. "The Sources of Poe's 'The Pit and the Pendulum,' " *MLN*, XXIV (1929), 349–56.

Clough, Wilson O. "The Use of Color Words by Edgar Allan Poe," *PMLA*, XLV (1930), 598–613.

Coad, Oral S. "The Meaning of Poe's 'Eldorado,' " *MLN*, LIX (1944), 59–61.

Coburn, Frederick. "Poe as Seen by the Brother of 'Annie,'" *NEQ*, XVL (1943), 468–76.

Cohen, B. B., and Lucian Cohen. "Poe and Griswold Once More," *AL*, XXXIV (1962), 97–101.

Cohen, Hennig. "Roderick Usher's Tragic Struggle," *NCF*, XIV (1959), 270–72.

Colby, Robert A. "Poe's Philosophy of Composition," *UKCR*, XX (1954), 211–14.

Colton, Cullen B. "George Hooker Colton and the Publication of 'The Raven,'" *AL*, X (1938), 319–30.

Connolly, Thomas. "Poe's 'Ulalume,'" *Expl*, XXII (1963), Item 4.

Cooke, Alice L. "The Popular Conception of Edgar Allan Poe from 1850–1890," *UTSE*, No. 4226 (1942), 145–70.

Cooke, Arthur L. "Edgar Allan Poe—Critic," *Cornhill Mag*, CL (1934), 588–97.

Cooper, C. B. "Tintinnabulation," *MLN*, XLI (1926), 318.

Cowley, Malcolm. "Aidgarpo," *New Republic*, CXIII (1945), 607–10.

Cox, J. L. "Poe as Critic," *EJ*, XXI (1922), 757–63.

Crawford, Polly. "Lewis and Clark's *Expedition* as a Source of Poe's 'Journal of Julius Rodman,'" *UTSE*, XII (1932), 158–70.

Cruz Monclava, Lidio. "Edgar Allan Poe y Puerto Rico," *Asomante*, XIV (1958), 64–69.

Culver, F. B. "Lineage of Edgar Allan Poe and the Complex Pattern of the Family Genealogy," *Md Hist Mag*, XXXVII (1942), 420–22.

D'Agostino, Nemi. "Poe, Whitman, Dickinson," *Belfagor*, VIII (Sept 30, 1953), 517–38.

Dameron, J. L. "Another 'Raven' for Edgar Allan Poe," *N & Q*, X (1963), 21–22.

———. "Poe and *Blackwood's* on the Art of Reviewing," *ESQ*, No. 31, 29–30.

———. "Poe at Mid-Century: Anglo-American Criticism, 1928–1960," *BSUF*, VIII (1967), 36–44.

———. "Poe's Reading of the British Periodicals," *MissQ*, XVIII (1964–65), 19–25.

———. "Schiller's 'Das Lied Vonder Glocke' as a Source of Poe's 'The Bells,'" *N & Q*, XIV, 368–69.

———, and Louis C. Stagg. "An Index to Poe's Critical Vocabulary," *ESQ*, XLVI, 1–50.

Daniel, Robert. "Poe's Detective God," *Furioso*, VI (1951), 45–54.

Danner, Richard. "The Poe-Matthews Theory of the American Short Story," *BSUF*, VIII (1967), 45–50.

Darnall, F. M. "The Americanism of Edgar Allan Poe," *EJ*, XVI (1927), 185–92.

Daughrity, K. L. "Notes: Poe and *Blackwood's*," *AL*, II (1930), 289–92.

———. "Poe's 'Quiz on Willis,'" *AL*, V (1933), 55–62.

Davidson, Frank. "A Note on Poe's 'Berenice,'" *AL*, XI (1939), 212–13.

Davis, Jeff. "The Lady Madeline as Symbol," *The Annotator* (Purdue), No. 2 (Ap, 1954), 8–11.

Davis, Richard B. "Moncure D. Conway Looks at Edgar Poe—Through Dr. Griswold," *MissQ*, XVIII (1964–65), 12–18.

———. "Poe and William Wirt," *AL*, XVI (1944), 212–20.

Dedman, Francis B. "An Additional Source of Poe's 'The Cask of Amontillado,'" *N & Q*, CXCVII (1952), 212–14.

———. "'The Cask of Amontillado' and the War of the Literati," *MLQ*, XV (1954), 137–46.

———. "A Checklist of Poe's Works in Book Form Published in the British Isles," *BBDI*, XXI, 16–20.

———. "Paul Hamilton Hayne and the Poe Westminster Memorial," *Md Hist Mag*, XLV (1950), 149–51.

———. "Poe in Drama, Fiction, and Poetry," *BBDI*, XXI, 107–14.

———. "Poe's Libel Suit Against T. D. English," *BPLQ*, V (1953), 31–37.

———. "The War of the Literati: Documents of the Legal Phase," *N & Q*, CXCVIII (1953), 303–308.

———. "Willis and Morris Add a Partner—and Poe," *N & Q*, CXCVIII (1953), 253–54.

———. "The Word 'Tintinnabulation' and a Source for Poe's 'The Bells,'" *N & Q*, CXCVI (1951), 520–21.

De Mille, G. E. "Poe as Critic," *Am Mer*, IV (1925), 433–40.

Dietz, F. M. "Poe's First and Final Love," *So Lit Mess*, V (1943), 38–47.

Di Marco, Sergio, "*Eureka* di Edgar Allan Poe," *RLMC*, XVII (1964), 265–85.

Diskin, Patrick. "Poe, Le Fanu, and the Sealed Room Mystery," *N & Q*, XIII (1966), 337–39.

Doherty, Edward. " 'The Spectacles': The Lost Short Story by Edgar Allan Poe," *Liberty*, XV (Sept 24, 1938), 12–14.

Dowdey, Clifford. "Poe's Last Visit to Richmond," *AH*, VII (Ap, 1956), 22–25, 96–97.

Dubois, A. E. "The Jazz Bells of Poe," *CE*, II (1940), 230–44.

———. "Poe and *Lolita*," *CEA*, XXVI (1964), 7.

Dudley, Fred A. "*Tintinnabulation*: And a Source of Poe's 'The Bells,'" *AL*, IV (1932), 296–300.

Duffy, Charles. "Poe's Mother-in-Law: Two Letters to Bayard Taylor," *Am N & Q*, II (1943), 148.

Durham, Frank M. "A Possible Relationship Between Poe's 'To Helen' and Milton's *Paradise Lost*," *AL*, XVI (1945), 340–43.

Eastman, Max. "Poe, Whitman et la poésie des temps nouveaux," *Europe*, XV (1927), 443–62.

Eaves, T. C. "Poe's Last Visit to Philadelphia," *AL*, XXVI (1954), 44–51.

Edgerton, Kathleen. "The Lecturing of Edgar Allan Poe," *SSJ*, XXVIII (1963), 268–73.

Edmunds, A. J. "German Translations of Poe's 'Raven,' " *N & Q*, CLXXIV (1938), 106.

Eliot, T. S. "From Poe to Valéry," *HudR*, II (1949), 327–42.

———. "Note sur Mallarmé et Poe," *NRF*, XIV (1926), 524–26.

———. "Review of Krutch's *Israfel*," *Nation and Athenaeum*, XLI (1927), 219.

Engel, Claire-Eliane. "L'Etat des travaux sur Poe en France," *MP*, XXIX (1932), 482–88.

Englekirk, J. E. " 'My Nightmare'—The Last Tale by Poe," *PMLA*, LII (1937), 511–27.

———. " 'The Raven' in Spanish America," *Span Rev*, I (1934).

———. "The Song of Hollands . . ." *New Mex Qt*, I (1931), 147–69.

Engstrom, Alfred. "Chateaubriand's *Itinéraire de Paris à Jerusalem* and Poe's 'The Assignation,' " *MLN*, LXIX (1954), 506–507.

———. "Poe, Leconte de Lisle, and Tzara's Formula for Poetry," *MLN*, LXXIII (1958), 434–36.

Evans, Mary G. "Poe in Amity Street," *Md Hist Mag*, XXXVI (1941), 363–80.

Evans, Oliver. "Infernal Illumination in Poe," *MLN*, LXXV (1960), 295–97.

Fagin, N. B. "Edgar Allan Poe," *SAQ*, LI (1952), 276–85.

———. "Poe—Drama Critic," *Theatre Annual*, 1946, 23–28.

Felheim, M. "The Cask of Amontillado," *N & Q*, n.s., I (1954), 447–48.

Ferguson, J. D. L. "Charles Hine and His Portrait of Poe," *AL*, III (1932), 465–70.

Fiedler, Leslie A. "Edgar Allan Poe and the Invention of the American Writer," *ChiR*, XIII (1959), 80–86.

Flanagan, Thomas. "The Life and Early Death of the Detective Story," *CUF*, I (1957), 7–10.

Foote, Dorothy N. "Poe's 'The Cask of Amontillado,' " *Expl*, XX, Item 27.

Forclaz, Roger. "Un voyage aux frontières de l'inconnu: *Les Aventures d'*A.G. *Pym*, d'Edgar Poe," *Etudes de Lettres*, VII (1964), 46–58.

Forsythe, Robert S. "Poe's 'Nevermore': A Note," *AL*, VII (1936), 439–52.

Fossum, Robert. "Poe's 'The Cask of Amontillado,' " *Expl*, XVII (1958), Item 16.

Foster, Edward F. "A Study of Grim Humor in the Works of Poe, Melville, and Twain," *DA*, XVII, 1761–62.

Fox, Hugh B., Jr. "Poe and Cosmology . . ." *DA*, XIX, 138.

Françon, Marcel. "Poe et Baudelaire," *PMLA*, LX (1945), 841–59.

Frank, Max. "Melville und Poe . . ." *Kleine Beitragë* (21), 19–23.

Freeman, Fred B., Jr. "The Identity of Poe's 'Miss B,' " *AL*, XXXIX, 389–91.

French, John C. "The Day of Poe's Burial," Baltimore *Sun,* June 3, 1949, 14.

——. "Poe's Literary Baltimore," *Md Hist Mag,* XXXII (1937), 101–12.

French, Warren. "T. S. Arthur: An Unexpected Champion of Poe," *TSLL,* V (1960), 35–41.

Friedman, William. "Edgar Allan Poe, Cryptographer," *AL,* VIII (1936), 266–80.

Fussell, Edwin. "Poe's 'Raven': or, How to Concoct a Popular Poem From Almost Nothing at All," *ELN,* II (1964), 36–39.

Galinsky, Hans. "Beharrende Strukturzüge im Wandel eines Jahrhunderts amerikanischer Kurzgeschichte (dargelegt an E. A. Poe's 'The Mask of the Red Death' and Hemingway's 'The Killers')," *NS,* 1958, 5–45.

Gargano, James W. "'The Black Cat': Perverseness Reconsidered," *TSLL,* II (1960), 172–78.

‣ ——. "'The Cask of Amontillado': A Masquerade of Motive and Identity," *SSF,* IV (1967), 119–26.

‣ ——. "Poe's 'Ligeia': Dream and Destruction," *CE,* XXIII (1962), 337–42.

——. "Poe's 'To Helen,'" *MLN,* LXXV (1960), 652–53.

——. "The Question of Poe's Narrators," *CE,* XXV (1963), 177–81.

Garnett, R. S. "The Mystery of Edgar Allan Poe," *Blackwood's,* CCXXVII (1930), 235–98.

Garrison, Joseph M. "The Function of Terror in the Works of Edgar Allan Poe," *AQ,* XVIII (1966), 136–50.

‣ Gerber, Gerald. "Additional Sources for 'The Masque of the Red Death,'" *AL,* XXXVII (1965–66), 52–54.

Ghiselin, Brewster. "Reading Sprung Rhythms," *Poetry,* LXX (May, 1947), 86–93.

Ghysbrecht, P. F. R. M., and R. J. G. Venneman. "Een fantasieproduct, 'The Raven' van E. A. Poe," *RLV*, XXII (1956), 79–84.

Giaccari, Ada. "La fortune di E. A. Poe in Italia," *SA*, V (1959), 91–118.

———. "Poe nella critica italiane," *SA*, V (1959), 51–89.

Gimbel, Richard. " 'Quoth the Raven': A Catalogue of the Exhibition" (from the collections of H. B. Marten and Richard Gimbel), *YULG*, XXXIII (1959), 139–89.

Gold, Joseph. "Reconstructing the 'House of Usher,'" *ESQ*, XXXVII (1964), 74–76.

Goodwin, K. L. "Roderick Usher's Overrated Knowledge," *NCF*, XVI (1961), 173–75.

Gordon, John D. "Edgar Allan Poe. An Exhibition on the Centenary of His Death, Oct. 7, 1849. A Catalog of First Editions, etc., from the Berg Collection," *BNYPL*, LIII (Oct, 1949), 471–91.

Grava, Arnolds. "L'aspect métaphysique du mal dans l'oeuvre littéraire de Charles Baudelaire et d'Edgar Poe," *DA*, XIV, 1238.

Gravely, W. H., Jr. "Christopher North and the Genesis of 'The Raven,'" *PMLA*, LXVI (1951), 149–61.

———. "An Incipient Libel Suit Involving Poe," *MLN*, LX (1945), 308–11.

———. "Thomas Dunn English's *Walter Woofe*—A Reply to "A Minor Poe Mystery,'" *PULC*, V (1944), 108–14.

Gray, John W. "The Public Reading of Edgar Allan Poe," *SSJ*, XXVIII (1963), 109–15.

Greenlaw, Edwin. "Poe in the Light of Literary History," *Johns Hopkins Alumni Mag*, XVIII (1930), 273–90.

Gregory, Horace. "Within the Private View: A Note on Re-reading the Poetry of Edgar Allan Poe," *PR*, X (1943), 263–74.

Griffith, Clark. "Poe's 'Ligeia' and the English Romantics," *UTQ*, XXIV (1954), 8–25.

Griggs, E. L. "Five Sources of Poe's 'Pinakidia,'" *AL*, I (1929), 196–99.

Gross, Seymour. "Poe's Revision of 'The Oval Portrait,'" *MLN*, LXXIV (1959), 16–20.

Grubb, Gerald. "The Personal and Literary Relationships of Dickens and Poe," *NCF*, V (1950), 101–20, 209–21.

Guilds, John C. "Poe's 'MS. Found in a Bottle': A Possible Source," *N & Q*, III (1956), 452.

———. "Poe's Vaults Again," *N & Q*, IV (1957), 220–21.

Gwynn, Frederick L. "Rappaccini's Daughter," *NCF*, VII, 217–18.

Hafley, James. "Malice in Wonderland" (Influence of "America" on "Oval Portrait" and James's *Portrait of a Lady*), *ArQ*, XV (1959), 5–17.

———. "A Tour of the House of Usher," *ESQ*, No. 31, 18–20.

Hagemann, E. R. "Two 'Lost' Letters by Poe . . ." *AL*, XXVIII (1957), 507–10.

Halliburton, David G. "The Grotesque in American Literature: Poe, Hawthorne, and Melville," *DA*, XXVII, 3840A–41A.

Halline, A. G. "Moral and Religious Concepts in Poe," *Bucknell Univ Stud*, II, 1951.

Hamilton, Robert. "Poe and the Imagination," *QR*, CCXXVIII (1950), 514–25.

Harbert, Earl W. "A New Poe Letter," *AL*, XXXV (1963), 80–81.

Hartley, Lodwick. "From Crazy Castle to the House of Usher: A Note Toward a Source," *SSF*, II (1965), 256–61.

Hassel, J. W. "The Problem of Realism in 'The Gold Bug,' " *AL*, XXV (1953), 179–92.

Hatvary, George. "Horace Dinney Wallace: A Study in Self-Destruction," *PULC*, XXV (1964), 137–49.

———. "Poe's Borrowings from H. D. Wallace," *AL*, XXXVIII (1966), 365–72.

Haviland, Thomas. "How Well Did Poe Know Milton?" *PMLA*, LXIX (1954), 841–60.

Hawkins, John. "Poe's 'The Murders in the Rue Morgue,' " *Expl*, XXIII (1965), Item 49.

Haycraft, Howard. "Poe's 'Purloined Letter,' " *PBSA*, LVI (1962), 486–87.

Hayford, Harrison. "Poe in *The Confidence Man*," *NCF*, XIV (Dec, 1959), 207–18.

Heartman, Charles F. "The Curse of Edgar Allan Poe," *ABC*, IV (1933), 45–49.

Heintzelman, Arthur. "Legros' Illustrations for Poe's *Tales*," *BPLQ*, VIII (1956), 43–48.

Hill, John S. "The Dual Hallucination in 'The Fall of the House of Usher,' " *SWR*, XLVIII (1963), 396–402.

———. "Poe's 'Fall of the House of Usher' and Frank Norris' Early Short Stories," *HLQ*, XXVI (1962), 111–12.

Hindus, Milton. "Whitman and Poe: A Note," *WWN*, III (Mar, 1957), 5–6.

Hirsh, David H. "Another Source for Poe's 'The Duc De L'Omelette,' " *AL*, XXXVIII (1966), 532–36.

Hoagland, Clayton. "The Universe of Eureka: A Comparison of the Theories of Eddington and Poe," *So Lit Mess*, I (1939), 307–13.

Hoffman, Michael J. "The House of Usher and Negative Romanticism," *SIR*, IV, 158–68.

Hofrichter, Laura. "From Poe to Kafka," *UTQ*, XXIX (1960), 405–19.

Holsapple, Cortell K. " 'The Masque of the Red Death' and *I Promessi Sposi,*" *Univ of Texas Pub,* No. 3826, *Studies in English* (1938), 137–39.

———. "Poe and Conradus," *AL,* IV (1932), 62–66.

Holt, Palmer C. "Notes on Poe's 'To Science,' 'To Helen,' and 'Ulalume,' " *BNYPL,* LXIII (1959), 568–70.

———. "Poe and H. N. Coleridge's *Greek Classic Poets*: 'Pinakidia,' 'Politian,' and 'Morella' Sources," *AL,* XXXIV (1962), 8–30.

Hoole, W. S. "Poe in Charleston, S. C.," *AL,* VI (1934), 78–80.

Hubbell, Jay B. "Charles Chancey Burr: Friend of Poe," *PMLA,* LXIX (1954), 833–40.

———. " 'O, Tempora! O, Mores!': A Juvenile Poem by Edgar Poe," *UCSLL,* Series B, II (1945), 314–21.

———. "Poe and the Southern Literary Tradition," *TSLL,* II (1960), 151–71.

———. "Poe's Mother: With A Note on John Allan," *WMQ,* XXI (1941), 250–54.

Hudson, Ruth L. "Poe and Disraeli," *AL,* VIII (1937), 402–16.

———. "Poe's Craftsmanship in the Short Story," *DA,* 1935, 8–11.

Hughes, David. "The Influence of Poe," *Fortnightly,* n.s., No. CMLXIV (1949), 342–43.

Hungerford, Edward. "Poe and Phrenology," *AL,* II (1930), 209–31.

Hunter, William B., Jr. "Poe's 'The Sleeper' and *Macbeth,*" *AL,* XX (1948), 55–57.

Huntress, Keith. "Another Source for Poe's *Arthur Gordon Pym,*" *AL,* XVI (1944), 19–25.

Hurley, Leonard B. "A New Note in the War of the Literati," *AL,* VII (1936), 376–94.

Hutcherson, Dudley R. *"The Philadelphia Saturday Museum* Text of Poe's Poems," AL, V (1933), 36–48.

———. "Poe's Reputation in England and America, 1850–1909," AL, XIV (1942), 211–33.

Huxley, Aldous. "Vulgarity in Literature," *SatR*, VII (Sept 27, 1930), 158–59.

"Israfel in the Laboratory," *TLS*, No. 2488 (Oct. 7, 1949), 648.

Jackson, David K. "Four of Poe's Critiques in the Baltimore Newspapers," *MLN*, L (1935), 251–56.

———. "Poe and the Messenger," *So Lit Mess*, I (1939), 5–11.

———. "Poe Notes: 'Pinakidia' and 'Some Ancient Greek Authors,' " AL, V (1933), 258–67.

———. "Poe's Knowledge of Law during the *Messenger* Period: Some Comments On Chapter II of Margaret Alterton's *Origins of Poe's Critical Theory*," AL, X (1938), 331–39.

———. "Some Unpublished Letters of T. W. White to Lucian Minor" (forty-six letters by the owner of the *Southern Literary Messenger* to his editorial advisers), *Tyler's Quar Hist* and *General Mag*, XVII (1936), 224–43; XVIII (1937) 32–48.

Jackson, Joseph. "George Lippard: Misunderstood Man of Letters," *Pa Mag of Hist and Biog*, LIX (Oct, 1935), 376–91.

Jacobs, Robert D. "Poe Among the Virginians," *VMHB*, LXVII (1958), 30–48.

———. "Poe and the Agrarian Critics," *Hopkins Rev*, V (1952), 43–54.

———. "Poe as a Literary Critic: A Teaching," *ESQ*, No. 31, 7–11.

———. "Poe's Earthly Paradise," AQ, XII (1960), 404–13.

———. "Rhetoric in Southern Writing: Poe," *GaR*, XII, 76–79.

Jones, H. M. "Poe, 'The Raven,' and the Anonymous Young Man," *WHR*, IX (1955), 127–38.

Jones, Joe J. "Poe's 'Nicean Barks,' " *AL*, II (1931), 433–38.

Jones, Joseph. " 'The Raven': Another Source of Poe's Poem," *AL*, XXX (1958), 185–93.

Jones, Louis C. "A Margaret Fuller Letter to Elizabeth Barrett Browning" (about Poe), *AL*, IX (1937), 70–71.

Jones, P. M. "Poe and Baudelaire: the 'Affinity,' " *MLR*, XL (1945), 279–83.

———. "Poe, Baudelaire, and Mallarmé: A Problem of Literary Judgment," *MLR*, XXXIX (1944), 236–46.

Jones, Rhys. "The Influence of Edgar Allan Poe on Paul Valéry, prior to 1900," *CLS*, XXI–XXII (1946), 10–15.

Kane, Margaret. "Edgar Allan Poe and Architecture," *SR*, XLI (1932), 149–60.

Keefer, T. F. " 'The City in the Sea': A Re-Examination," *CE*, XXV (1964), 436–39.

Kelly, George. "Poe's Theory of Beauty," *AL*, XXVII (1956), 521–36.

———. "Poe's Theory of Unity," *PQ*, XXXVII (1958), 34–44.

Kendall, Lyle H., Jr. "The Vampire Motif in 'The Fall of the House of Usher,' " *CE*, XXIV (1963), 450–53.

Kennedy, R. C. "The Poems and Short Stories of Edgar Allan Poe: Their Composition, Publication, and Reception," *DA*, XXII, 1158.

Kern, Alfred A. "Poe's Theory of Poetry," *Bull Randolf-Macon Coll*, XIX (1932), 10–13.

Kiehl, James. "The Valley of Unrest: A Major Metaphor in the Poetry of Poe," *Thoth*, V (1964), 42–52.

Kime, Wayne R. "Poe's Use of Irving's *Astoria* in 'The Journal of Julius Rodman,'" AL, XL (1968), 215–22.

King, Lucille. "Notes on Poe's Sources," *UTSE*, X (1930), 128–34.

Knox, Robert. " 'La Mariposa Negra' and 'The Raven,'" *Symposium*, XI (1957), 111–16.

Korponay, Béla. "Edgar Allan Poe in Hungary," *HSE*, I (1963), 43–62.

Krappe, Edith S. "A Possible Source for Poe's 'The Tell-Tale Heart' and 'The Black Cat,'" AL, XII (1940), 84–88.

Kremenliev, E. B. "The Literary Uses of Astronomy in the Writings of Edgar Allan Poe," DA, XXIV, 4176.

Kronegger, M. E. "Joyce's Debt to Poe and the French Symbolists," *RLC*, XXXIX (1965), 243–54.

———. "The Theory of Unity and Effect in the Works of E. A. Poe and James Joyce," *RLC*, XL (1966), 226–34.

Krutch, Joseph Wood. "His Nightmares Go On For Evermore," *NYTBR*, Jan 18, 1959, 1, 22.

———. "The Strange Case Of Poe," *Am Mer*, VI (1925), 349–56.

Kühnelt, Harro H. "Die Anfnahme und Verbreitung von E. A. Poes Werken im Deutschen," *Festschrift fur Walther Fischer* (1962), 195–224.

———. "E. A. Poe und Alfred Kubin—zwei kunstlerische Gestalter des Grauens," *Festschrift* (1955), 121–41.

———. "T. S. Eliot als Poe-Kritiker." *NS*, Heft 3, 105–112.

Lafleur, L. J. "Edgar Allan Poe as Philosopher," *Person*, XXII (1941), 401–405.

Laser, Marvin. "The Growth and Structure of Poe's Concept of Beauty," *ELH*, XV (1948), 69–84.

———. "Poe's Critical Theories—Sense or Nonsense," *ESQ*, No. 31, 20–23.

Lauber, John. " 'Ligeia' and Its Critics: A Plea for Liberalism," *Stud in Short Fiction,* IV (1966), 28–32.

Lauter, Paul. "The Narrator of 'The Blessed Damozel,' " *MLN,* LXXIII (1958), 344–48.

Lauvrière, Emile. "Edgar Poe et le Freudisme," *La Grande Revue,* CXLII (1933), 565–87.

Laverty, Carroll D. "The Death's-Head on the Gold-Bug," *AL,* XII (1940), 88–91.

———. "A Note on Poe in 1838," *MLN,* LXIV (1949), 174–76.

———. "Poe in 1847," *AL,* XX (1948), 163–68.

———. "Poe in His Place: In His Time," *ESQ,* No. 31, 23–25.

Lawson, Lewis A. "Poe's Conception of the Grotesque," *MissQ,* XIX (1966), 200–205.

Leary, Lewis. "Poe's 'Ulalume,' " *Expl,* VI (1948), 25.

Lee, Muna. "Brother of Poe (José Ascunción Silva)," *SWR,* XI (1926), 305–12.

Lemonnier, Léon. "Edgar et les parnassiens françaises," *RLC,* IX (1929), 728–36.

———. "Edgar Poe et le Roman scientific française," *La Grande Rev,* LXXXIII (1930), 214–23.

———. "Edgar Poe et le théâtre de mystère et de terreur," *La Grande Rev,* LXXX (1929), 379–96.

———. "L'Influence d'Edgar Poe sur les conteurs françaises symbolistes et décadents," *RLC,* XIII (1933), 102–34.

———. "L'Influence d'Edgar Poe sur quelque conteurs réalistes," *RLC,* XI (1931), 451–65.

———. "L'Influence d'Edgar Poe sur Villiers de l'Isle-Adam," *Mercure de France,* 246 (1933), 604–19.

Levine, Stuart G. "Poe's *Julius Rodman*: Judaism, Plagiarism, and the Wild West," *MWQ,* I (1960), 245–59.

———. " 'The Proper Spirit': A Study of the Prose Fiction of Edgar Poe," *DA*, XIX, 1742.

Lewis, C. L. "Edgar Allan Poe and the Sea," *So Lit Mess*, III (1941), 5–10.

Ligon, John F. "On Desperate Seas: A Study of Poe's Imaginary Journeys," *DA*, XXII, 3201–3202.

Lind, Sidney E. "Poe and Mesmerism," *PMLA*, LXII (1947), 1077–94.

Link, Franz H. " 'Discovery' und 'Destruction' . . . 'MS. Found in a Bottle,' " *NS*, 1961, 27–38.

———. "Edgar Allan Poes 'Ligeia' und das Paradoxon der Modernen Dichtung," *DVLG*, XXXVII (1963), 363–76.

Lloyd, J. A. T. "Who Wrote 'English Notes'?" *Colophon*, I (1935), 107–18.

Lockspeiser, Edward. "Debussy and Edgar Allan Poe," *Listener*, LXVIII (1962), 609–10.

Lograsso, Angeline H. "Poe's Piero Maroncelli," *PMLA*, LVIII (1943), 780–89.

Lubbers, Klaus. "Poe's 'The Conqueror Worm,' " *AL*, XXXIX (1967), 375–79.

Lubell, Albert J. "Poe and A. W. Schlegel," *JEGP*, LII (1953), 1–12.

Lynch, James J. "The Devil in the Writings of Irving, Hawthorne, and Poe," *NYFQ*, VIII, 111–31.

Lyons, Nathan. "Kafka and Poe, and Hope," *MinnR*, V (1965), 158–68.

Mabbott, Thomas O. "Additions to 'A List of Poe's Tales,' " *N & Q*, CLXXXIII (1942), 163–64.

———. "Allusions to a Spanish Joke in Poe's 'A Valentine,' " *N & Q*, CLXIX (1935), 189.

———. "Antediluvian Antiquities: A Curiosity of American

Literature and a Source of Poe's," *Am Coll*, IV (1927), 124–26.

———. "The Astrological Symbolism of Poe's 'Ulalume,' " *N & Q*, CLXI (1931), 27.

———. "Dumas on Poe's Visit to Paris," NY *Times*, Dec 22, 1929, 5.

———. "An Early Discussion of Poe," *N & Q*, CXCI (1947), 102.

———. "Echoes of Poe in Rossetti's 'Beryl Song,' " *N & Q*, CLXVIII (1935), 77.

———. "English Publications of Poe's 'Valdemar Case,' " *N & Q*, CLXXXIII (1942), 311–12.

———. "Evidence That Poe Knew Greek," *N & Q*, CLXXXV (1943), 39–40.

———. "The First Publication of Poe's 'Raven,' " *BNYPL*, XLVII (1943), 581–84.

———. "German Translations of Poe's 'Raven,' " *N & Q*, CLXXIV (1938), 88.

———. "Greeley's Estimate of Poe," *Autograph Album*, I (1933), 14–16.

———. "Joel Chandler Harris: A Debt to Poe," *N & Q*, CLXVI (1935), 151–52.

———. "Letters from Mary E. Hewitt to Poe," *Christmas Books* (Hunter College), Dec, 1937, 116–21.

———. "A List of Books from Poe's Library," *N & Q*, n.s., II (1955), 222–23.

———. "A Lost Jingle by Poe," *N & Q*, CLXXIX (1940), 371.

———. "Newly Found Verses Ascribed to Poe," *N & Q*, III (1956), 122.

———. "Newly-Identified Reviews by Edgar Poe," *N & Q*, CLXIII (1932), 441.

——. "Newly-Identified Verses by Poe," *N & Q*, CLXXVII (1939), 77–78.

——. "Numismatic References of Three American Writers," *Numismatist*, XLVI (Nov, 1933), 688.

——. "On Poe's 'Tales of the Folio Club,'" *Sew Rev*, XXXVI (1928), 171–76.

——. "Palindromes (and Edgar Allan Poe)," *N & Q*, CXCI (1947), 238–39.

——. "Poe and Ash Upson," *N & Q*, CLXXII (1937), 330–31.

——. "Poe and Dr. Lardner," *Am N & Q*, III (1943), 115–17.

——. "Poe and the Artist John P. Frankenstein," *N & Q*, CLXXXII (1942), 31–32.

——. "Poe and the Philadelphia Irish Citizen," *Jour Am Irish Hist Soc*, XXIX (1930–31), 121–31.

——. "Poe Letter (1848) about 'The Raven,'" *Am N & Q*, III, 67.

——. "A Poem Wrongly Ascribed to Poe," *N & Q*, XIV, 367–68.

——. "Poe on Intemperance," *N & Q*, CLXXXII (1942), 34–35.

——. "Poe's Balloon Hoax," *New York Sun*, Jan 23, 1943, 6.

——. "Poe's 'Israfel,'" *Expl*, II (1944), Item 57.

——. "Poe's 'The Man That Was Used Up,'" *Expl*, XXV, Item 70.

——. "Poe's Obscure Contemporaries," *Am N & Q*, I (1942), 166–77.

——. "Poe's Original Conundrums," *N & Q*, CLXXXIV (1943), 328–29.

——. "Poe's 'Raven': First Inclusion in a Book," *N & Q*, CLXXXV (1943), 225.

———. "Poe's Tale, 'The Lighthouse,' " *N & Q*, CLXXXII (1942), 226–27.

———. "Poe's 'The Cask of Amontillado,' " *Expl*, XXV (1966), Item 30.

———. "Poe's 'The Fall of the House of Usher,' " *Expl*, XV (1956), Item 7.

———. "Poe's 'The Sleeper' Again," *AL*, XXI (1949), 339–40.

———. "Poe's 'To Helen,' " *Expl*, I (1943), 60.

———. "Poe's 'Ulalume,' " *N & Q*, CLXIV (1933), 143.

———. "Poe's 'Ulalume,' " *Expl*, I (1943), 1–2.

———. "Poe's 'Ulalume,' " *Expl*, VI (1948), 57.

———. "Poe's Vaults," *N & Q*, CXCVIII (1953), 542–43.

———. "Poe's Word 'Porphyrogene,' " *N & Q*, CLXXVII (1939), 403.

———. "Poe's Word 'Tintinnabulation,' " *N & Q*, CLXXV (1938), 387.

———. "Puckle and Poe," *N & Q*, CLXIV (1933), 205–206.

———. "A Review of Lowell's Magazine" (Poe on Lowell's *Pioneer*), *N & Q*, CLXXVIII (1941), 457–58.

———. "The Source of Poe's Motto for 'The Gold Bug,' " *N & Q*, CXCVIII (1953), 68.

———. "The Source of the Title of Poe's 'Morella,' " *N & Q*, CLXXII (1937), 26–27.

———. "The Sources of Poe's 'Eldorado,' " *MLN*, LX (1945), 312–14.

———. "The Text of Poe's Play, *Politian*," *N & Q*, CXXXIX (1945), 14.

———. "Ullahanna—A Literary Ghost," *Am N & Q*, I (1941), 83.

———. "An Unpublished Letter To Poe," *N & Q*, CLXXIV (1938), 385.

———. "Unrecorded Texts of Two Poe Poems" ("To One in Paradise" and "Lenore"), *Am N & Q*, VIII (1948), 67–68.

———. "The Writing of Poe's 'The Bells,'" *Am N & Q*, II (1942), 110.

McAleer, John J. "Poe and Gothic Elements in *Moby Dick*," *ESQ*, No. 27, 34.

McCorison, M. A. "An Unpublished Poe Letter" (to Duyckinck), *AL*, XXXII (1961), 455–56.

MacDonald, Dwight. "Masscult and Midcult," *PR*, XXVII (1960), 203–33, 589–630.

McDowell, Tremaine. "Edgar Allan Poe and Willaim Cullen Bryant," *PQ*, XVI (1937), 83–84.

McElderry, B. R., Jr. "The Edgar Allan Poe Collection," *Univ So Cal Lib Bul*, No. 4, 4–6.

———. "Poe's Concept of the Soul," *N & Q*, n.s., II (1955), 173–74.

McKeithan, D. M. "Two Sources of Poe's *Narrative of Arthur Gordon Pym*," *UTSE*, XIII (1933), 116–37.

McLean, Frank. "The Conditions Under Which Poe Did His Imaginative Work," *SR*, XXXIV (1926), 184–95.

McNeal, Thomas. "Poe's 'Zenobia': An Early Satire on Margaret Fuller," *MLQ*, XI (1950), 215–16.

Maddison, Carol H. "Poe's *Eureka*," *TSLL*, II (1960), 350–67.

Marchand, Ernest. "Poe as Social Critic," *AL*, VI (1934), 28–43.

Marks, Alfred. "Two Rodericks and Two Worms: 'Egotism; or, The Bosom Serpent'" (Poe and Hawthorne), *PMLA*, LXXIV (1959), 607–12.

Marks, Emerson. "Poe as Literary Theorist: A Reappraisal," *AL*, XXXIII (1961), 296–306.

Martin, Terence. "The Imagination at Play: Edgar Allan Poe," *KR*, XXVIII (1966), 194–209.

Mason, Leo. "Poe—Script," *Dickinsian*, XLII (1946), 79–81.

Matthews, Joseph C. "Did Poe Read Dante?" *Univ of Texas Pub*, No. 3826, *Studies in English* (1938), 123–36.

Menander (pseud.). "The Aesthetic of Poe," *London TLS*, June 17, 1944, 291.

Mengeling, Marvin, and Frances Mengeling. "From Fancy to Failure: A Study of the Narrators in the Tales of Edgar Allan Poe," *UR*, XXXIII (1967), 293–98.

Miller, Arthur M. "The Influence of Edgar Allan Poe on Ambrose Bierce," *AL*, IV (1932), 130–50.

Miller, F. D. "The Basis for Poe's 'The Island of the Fay,' " *AL*, XIV (1942), 135–40.

Miller, James. " 'Ulalume' Resurrected," *PQ*, XXXIV (1955), 197–205.

Miller, John C. "A Poe Letter Re-Presented," *AL*, XXXV (1963), 359–61.

———. "Poe's English Biographer: John Henry Ingram, a Biographical Account . . ." *DA*, XIV, 2070–71.

———. "Poe's Sister Rosalie," *TSL*, VIII (1963), 107–17.

———. "An Unpublished Poe Letter," *AL*, XXVI (1955), 560–61.

Mohr, Franz. "The Influence of Eichendorff's 'Achnung and Gegenwart' on Poe's 'Masque of the Red Death,' " *MLQ*, X (1949), 3–15.

Monroe, Harriet. "Poe and Longfellow," *Poetry*, XXXIX (1927), 266–74.

Moon, S. "The Cask of Amontillado," *N & Q*, n.s., I (1954), 448.

Mooney, Stephen L. "The Comic in Poe's Fiction," *AL*, XXXIII (1962), 433–41.

———. "Comic Intent in Poe's Tales: Five Criteria," *MLN*, LXXVI (1961), 432–34.

———. "Poe's Gothic Wasteland," *SR*, LXX (1962), 261–83.

Moore, John R. "Poe, Scott, and 'The Murders in the Rue Morgue,'" *AL*, VIII (1936), 52–58.

———. "Poe's Reading of *Anne of Greirstein*," *AL*, XXII (1951), 493–96.

Moore, Rayburn. "A Note on Poe and the Sons of Temperance," *AL*, XXX (1958), 359–61.

Morley, Christopher. "The Allegory of Roderick Usher," *London TLS*, No. 2462 (Ap 9, 1949), 233.

Morrison, Claudia C. "Poe's 'Ligeia': An Analysis," *SSF*, IV, 234–44.

Moss, Sidney. "*Arthur Gordon Pym* or the Fallacy of Thematic Interpretation," *UR*, XXIII (1967), 299–306.

———. "A Conjecture Concerning the Writing of *Arthur Gordon Pym*," *SSF*, IV (1966), 83–85.

———. "Poe and His Nemesis—Lewis Gaylord Clark," *AL*, XXVIII (1956), 30–46.

———. "Poe and the Literary Cliques," *ABC*, VII (1957), 13–19.

———. "Poe and the Norman Leslie Incident," *AL*, XXV (1953), 293–306.

———. "Poe, Hiram Fuller, and The Duyckinck Circle," *ABC*, XVIII, ii, 8–18.

———. "Poe's Infamous Reputation: A Crux in the Biography," *ABC*, VIII (1958), xi, 3–10.

Mossop, D. J. "Poe's Theory of Pure Poetry," *DUJ*, XVII (1956), 60–67.

Moyne, Ernest J. "Did Edgar Allan Poe Lecture at Newart Academy?" *Delaware Notes*, 26th ser., 1–19.

Murphy, George D. "A Source for Ballistics in Poe," *Am N & Q*, IV (1966), 99.

Neal, Walter G., Jr. "The Source of Poe's 'Morella,' " *AL*, IX (1937), 237–39.

Nisbet, Ada B. "New Light on the Dickens-Poe Relationship," *NCF*, V (1951), 295–302.

Nordstedt, George. "Poe and Einstein," *Open Court*, XLIV (1930), 173–80.

———. "Prototype of 'The Raven,' " *No Am Rev*, CCIV (1927), 692–701.

Norman, Emma K. "Poe's Knowledge of Latin," *AL*, VI (1934), 72–77.

O'Donnell, Charles. "From Earth to Ether: Poe's Flight into Space," *PMLA*, LXXVII (1962), 85–91.

Olney, Clarke. "Edgar Allan Poe: Science Fiction Pioneer," *GaR*, XII (1958), 416–21.

Olson, Bruce. "Poe's Strategy in 'The Fall of the House of Usher,' " *MLN*, LXXV (1960), 556–59.

O'Neill, Edward H. "The Poe-Griswold-Harrison Texts of the 'Marginalia,' " *AL*, XV (1943), 238–50.

Oras, Ants. " 'The Bells' of Edgar Allan Poe and 'A Prophecy' by John Keats," *Apophoreta Tartuensia* (Stockholm), III, 17–44.

Ostrom, John W. "A Poe Correspondence Re-edited," *Americana*, XXXIV (1940), 409–46.

———. "Second Supplement to *The Letters* of Poe," *AL*, XXIX (1957), 79–86.

———. "Supplement to *The Letters* of Poe," *AL*, XXIV (1952), 358–66.

———. "Two 'Lost' Poe Letters," *Am N & Q*, I (1941), 68–69.

———. "Two Unpublished Poe Letters," *Americana*, XXXVI (1942), 67–71.

Parkes, Henry. "Poe, Hawthorne, Melville: An Essay in Sociological Criticism," *PR*, XVI (1949), 157–65.

Parks, Edd W. "Edgar Allan Poe como Critico," *Diario de São Paulo*, Oct 8, 1949, 3.

Pearce, D. "The Cask of Amontillado," *N & Q*, n.s., I (1954), 448–49.

Peters, H. F. "Ernst Jünger's Concern with Edgar Allan Poe," *CL*, X (1958), 144–49.

Peterson, D. W. "Poe's Grotesque Humor: A Study of the Grotesque Effects in His Humorous Tales," *DA*, XXIII, 3355–56.

Petriconi, Hellmuth. "Abenteurer und kein Ende II: Aventures d'Arthur Gordon Pym," *Romanistisches Jahrbuch*, XV (1964), 160–71.

Pettigrew, Richard C. "Poe's Rime," *AL*, IV (1932), 151–59.

———, and Marie M. Pettigrew. "A Reply to Floyd Stovall's Interpretation of 'Al Aaraaf,' " *AL*, VIII (1937), 439–45.

Philips, Edith. "The French of Edgar Allan Poe," *AS*, II (1927), 270–74.

Phillips, Elizabeth. "Edgar Allan Poe: The American Context," *DA*, XVIII, 2614–15.

———. "The Hocus-Pocus of *Lolita*" (Poe as inspiration for the novel), *L & P*, X (1960), 97–101.

Phillips, William L. "Poe's 'The Fall of the House of Usher,' " *Expl*, IX (1951), 29.

Pittman, Diana. "Key to the Mystery of Edgar Allan Poe," *So Lit Mess*, III (1941), 367–77, 418–24; IV (1942), 81–85, 143–68.

———. "Key to the Mystery of 'Ulalume,' " *So Lit Mess*, III (1941), 371–77.

Pollin, Burton. "Bulver-Lytton and 'The Tell-Tale Heart,' " *Am N & Q*, IV (1965), 7–8.

———. "New York City in the Tales of Poe," *Bronx County Hist Soc Jour*, II (Jan, 1965), 16–22.

———. "Poe and Godwin," *NCF*, XX (1965), 237–53.

———. "Poe as 'Miserrimus': From British Epitaph to American Epithet," *Rev de Langues Vivantes*, XXXIII, 347–61.

———. "Poe As Probable Author of 'Harper's Ferry,' " *AL*, XL (1968), 164–78.

———. "Poe's 'Von Kempelen and His Discovery': Sources and Significance," *Etudes Anglaises*, XX, 12–23.

———. "The 'Spectacles' of Poe—Sources and Significance," *AL*, XXXVII (1965–66), 185–90.

Posey, M. N. "Notes on Poe's 'Hans Pfaal,' " *MLN*, XLV (1930), 501–507.

Pound, Louise. "On Poe's 'The City in the Sea,' " *AL*, VI (1934), 22–27.

———. "Poe's 'The City in the Sea' Again," *AL*, VIII (1936), 70–71.

Praz, Mario. "Poe, genio d'esportazione," *Approdo*, IV (1958), iii, 3–15.

———. "Poe and Psychoanalysis (1933)," *SR*, LXVIII, 375–89.

Pritchard, John P. "Aristotle's *Poetics* and Certain American Critics," *Classical Weekly*, XXVIII (Jan 8, 1934), 81–85.

Pugh, Griffith. "Poe: An Induction," *EJ*, XLV (1956), 509–16.

Quarles, Diana. "Poe and International Copyright," *So Lit Mess*, III (1941), 438–44.

Quinn, Arthur H. "The Marriage of Poe's Parents," *AL*, XI (1939), 209–12.

Quinn, Patrick F. "Four Views of Edgar Poe," *Jahr fur Am*, V (1960), 138–46.

———. "The French Face of Edgar Poe." *DA*, XIV, 131–32.

———. "Poe's *Eureka* and Emerson's *Nature*," *ESQ*, No. 31, 4–7.

———. "Poe's Imaginary Voyage" (*Gordon Pym*), *HudR*, IV (1952), 562–86.

———. "The Profundities of Edgar Poe," *YFS*, No. 6, 3–13.

Rado, György. "The Works of E. A. Poe in Hungary," *Babel*, XII (1966), 21–22.

Ramakrishna, D. "The Conclusion of Poe's 'Ligeia,' " *ESQ*, XLVII, 69–70.

———. "Poe's *Eureka* and Hindu Philosophy," *ESQ*, XLVII, 28–32.

———. "Poe's 'Ligeia,' " *Expl*, XXV (1966), Item 19.

Ramsey, Paul. "Poe and Modern Art," *CAJ*, XVIII (1959), 210–15.

Randall, John H. "Poe's 'The Cask of Amontillado' and the Code of the Duello," *SGG*, V (1963), 175–84.

Rasor, C. L. "Possible Sources of 'The Cask of Amontillado,' " *Furman Stud*, XXXI (1949), 46–50.

Rauter, Herbert. "Edgar Allan Poe's 'The Man in the Crowd,' " *NS*, n.f., II (1962), 497–508.

Rea, Joy. "Classicism and Romanticism in Poe's 'Ligeia,' " *BSUF*, VIII (1967), 25–29.

———. "Poe's 'The Cask of Amontillado,' " *SSF*, IV (1966), 57–69.

Rede, Kenneth. "New Poe Manuscript," *Am Coll*, III (Dec, 1929), 100–102.

———. "Poe Notes: From An Investigator's Notebook," *AL*, V (1933), 49–54.

———. "Poe's Annie: Leaves from Lonesome Years," *Am Coll*, IV (Ap, 1927), 21–28.

Redmond, Catherine. "Edgar Allan Poe, Soldier," *Quartermaster Rev*, XVI (1937), 18–21, 73–74.

Reece, James. "New Light on Poe's 'The Masque of the Red Death,' " *MLN*, LXVIII (1953), 114–15.

Reilly, John E. "Poe in Imaginative Literature: A Study of American Drama, Fiction, and Poetry Devoted to Edgar Allan Poe or His Works," *DA*, XXVI, 6050.

Rein, David. "Poe and Mrs. Shelton," *AL*, XXVIII (1956), 225–27.

———. "Poe and Virginia Clemm," *BuR*, VII (1958), 207–16.

———. "Poe's Dreams," *AQ*, X (1958), 367–71.

———. "Poe's 'Introduction, XXXI–XXXIV' " *Expl*, XX (1961), Item 8.

Reiss, Edmund. "The Comic Setting of 'Hans Pfaal,' " *AL*, XXIX (1957), 306–309.

Rendall, V. "Dumas and Poe," *London TLS*, Nov 28, 1929.

Rhea, Robert L. "Some Observations on Poe's Origins," *UTSE*, X (1930), 135–46.

Rhodes, S. A. "The Influence of Poe on Baudelaire," *RR*, XVIII (1927), 329–33.

Richards, Irving T. "A New Poe Poem," *MLN*, XLII (1927), 158–62.

Richardson, C. F. "Poe's Doctrine of Effect," *UCPMP*, XI (1928), 179–86.

Ridgely, Joseph V., and Iola S. Haverstick. "Chartless Voyage: The Many Narratives of Arthur Gordon Pym," *TSLL*, VIII (1966), 63–80.

Robbins, J. A. "An Addition to Poe's 'Steamboat Letters,' " *N & Q*, X, 20–21.

———. "Edgar Poe and His Friends: A Sampler of Letters Written to Sarah Helen Whitman," *IUB*, No. 4 (1960), 5–45.

Roberts, W. "A Dumas Manuscript: Did Edgar Allan Poe Visit Paris?" *London TLS*, Nov 21, 1929.

Robertson, J. M. S. "The Genius of Poe," *Mod Qt*, III (1926), 274–84; IV (1927), 60–72.

Robinson, Arthur E. "Order and Sentience in 'The Fall of the House of Usher,'" *PMLA*, LXXVI (1961), 68–81.

Robinson, E. A. "Poe's 'The Tell-Tale Heart,'" *NCF*, XIX (1965), 365–78.

Roppolo, Joseph. "Meaning and the 'Masque of the Red Death,'" *TSE*, XIII (1963), 59–69.

Rosati, Salvatore. "La teoria dell'unità d'effetto in E. A. Poe e la sua portata critica," *Il Simbolismo* (59), 161–68.

Rossi, Sergio. "E. A. Poe e la Scapigliatura lombarda," *SA*, V (1959), 119–39.

Rothwell, Kenneth. "A Source for the Motto to Poe's 'William Wilson,'" *MLN*, LXXIV (1958), 297–98.

Rubin, Joseph J. "John Neal's Poetics as an Influence on Whitman and Poe," *N & Q*, XIV (1941), 359–62.

Runden, John. "Rossetti and a Poe Image," *N & Q*, V (1958), 257–58.

Ryan, Sylvester. "A Poe Oversight," *CE*, XI (1950), 408.

Saintsbury, George. "Edgar Allan Poe," *Dial*, LXXXIII (1927), 451–63.

Samuel, Dorothy. "Poe and Baudelaire: Parallels in Form and Symbol," *CLAJ*, III (1959), 88–105.

Samuels, Charles. "Usher's Fall; Poe's Rise," *GaR*, XVIII (1964), 208–16.

Sanderlin, W. S. "Poe's 'Eldorado' Again," *MLN*, LXXI (1956), 189–92.

Sandler, G. S. "Poe's Indebtedness to Locke . . .," *BUSE*, V (1961), 107–21.

San Juan, E., Jr. "The Form of Experience in the Poems of Edgar Allan Poe," *GaR*, XXI, 65–80.

Schick, J. S. "The Origin of 'The Cask of Amontillado,' " *AL*, VI (1934), 18–21.

———. "Poe and Jefferson," *VMHB*, LIV (1946), 316–20.

Schneider, Joseph. "French Appreciation of Edgar Allan Poe," *Cath Educ Rev*, XXV (1927), 427–37.

Schoettle, Elmer. "A Musician's Commentary on Poe's 'The Philosophy of Composition,' " *Forum H*, IV (1964), 14–15.

Schreiber, Carl F. "A Close-up of Poe," *SatR*, III (Oct 9, 1926), 165–67.

———. "The Donkey and the Elephant" (on slanderous remarks by Thomas Dunn English about Poe), *YULG*, XIX (1944), 17–19.

———. "Mr. Poe and His Conjurations Again" (Poe's reading of German), *Colophon*, Part II, May, 1930.

Schroeter, James. "A Misreading of Poe's 'Ligeia,' " *PMLA*, LXXVI (1961), 397–406.

Schubert, Leland. "James William Carling: Expressionist Illustrator of 'The Raven,' " *So Lit Mess*, IV (1942), 173–81.

Schwartz, W. L. "The Influence of Edgar Allan Poe on Judith Gautier," *MLN*, XLII (1927), 171–73.

Schwartzstein, Leonard. "Poe's Criticism of William W. Lord," *N & Q*, n.s., II (1955), 312.

Scudder, Harold. "Poe's 'Balloon Hoax,' " *AL*, XXI (1949), 179–90.

Seronsy, Cecil C. "Poe and 'Kubla Khan,' " *N & Q*, IV (1957), 219–20.

Shockley, M. S. *"Timur the Tartar* and Poe's *Tamerlane."* *PMLA*, LIV (1941), 1103–1106.

Simpson, Lewis P. "Poe and the Literary Vocation in America," *ESQ*, No. 31, 11–14.

Skaggs, Calvin L. "Narrative Point of View in Edgar Allan Poe's Criticism and Fiction," *DA*, XXVII, 3880A–81A.

Smith, Grace P. "Poe's 'Metzengerstein,' " *MLN*, XLVIII (1933), 356–59.

Smith, Herbert F. "Usher's Madness and Poe's Organicism: A Source," *AL*, XXXIX (1967), 379–89.

Smith, Julia. "A New Light on Poe," *So Lit Mess*, I (1939), 575–81.

Smithline, Arnold. *"Eureka*: Poe as Transcendentalist," *ESQ*, No. 39 (1965), 25–28.

Snell, George. "First of the New Critics," *QRL*, II, 333–40.

Snider, Harry Clark. "An Edition of the Poems in Poe's Lost Collection Based Largely on His Own Critical Principles," *DA*, XXIV, 3344.

Snow, Sinclair. "The Similarity of Poe's 'Eleonora' to Bernardin de Saint-Pierre's *Paul et Virginie*," *RomN*, V (1963), 40–44.

Snyder, Edward D. "Bowra on Poe: Corrections," *MLN*, LXVII (1952), 422–23.

———. "Poe and Amy Lowell," *MLN*, XLIII (1928), 152–53.

———. "Poe's Nicean Barks," *CJ*, XLVIII (1953), 159–69.

"Souvenirs of Poe's Last Visit to Richmond," *PULC*, XII (1951), 83–87.

Spaulding, K. A. "Poe's 'The Fall of the House of Usher,' " *Expl*, X (1952), 52.

Spitzer, Leo. "A Reinterpretation of 'The Fall of The House of Usher,' " *CL*, IV (1952), 351–63.

Spivey, Herman E. "Poe and Lewis Baylord Clark," *PMLA*, LIV (1939), 1124–32.

Starke, Aubrey. "Poe's Friend Reynolds," *AL*, XI, (1939), 152–59.

Starrett, Vincent. "One Who Knew Poe," *Bkm*, LXIV (1927), 196–201.

———. "A Poe Mystery Uncovered: The Lost Minerva Review Of *Al Aaraaf*," *SatR*, XXVI (May 1, 1943), 4–5.

Stauffer, Donald B. "Prose Style in the Fiction of Edgar Allan Poe," *DA*, XXIV, 2912.

———. "Style and Meaning in 'Ligeia' and 'William Wilson,' " *SSF*, II, 316–30.

Steele, Charles W. "Poe's 'The Cask of Amontillado,' " *Expl*, XVIII (1960), Item 43.

Stein, William B. "The Twin Motif in 'The Fall of the House of Usher,' " *MLN*, LXXV (1960), 109–11.

Stern, Madeline B. "Poe: 'The Mental Temperment' For Phrenologists," *AL*, XL (1968), 155–63.

Stern, Philip Van Doren. "The Strange Death of Edgar Allan Poe," *SRL*, Oct 15, 1949, 8–9.

Stewart, Charles. "A Pilfering by Poe," *Atlantic*, CII (Dec, 1958), 67–68.

Stockton, Eric W. "Celestial Inferno: Poe's 'The City in the Sea,' " *TSL*, VIII (1963), 99–106.

Stone, Edward. "Poe In and Out of Time," *ESQ*, No. 31, 14–17.

———. "Usher, Poquelin, and Miss Emily: The Progress of Southern Gothic," *GaR*, XIV (1960), 433–43.

Stovall, Floyd. "The Concious Art of Edgar Allan Poe," *CE*, XXIV (1963), 417–21.

———. "Edgar Poe and The University of Virginia," *VQR*, XLIII (1967), 297–317.

———. "An Interpretation of Poe's 'Al Aaraaf,' " *UTSE*, IX (1929), 106–33.

———. "Poe as a Poet of Ideas," *UTSE*, XI (1931), 56–62.

———. "Poe's Debt to Coleridge," *UTSE*, X (1930), 70–127.

———. "An Unpublished Poe Letter," *AL*, XXXVI, 514–15.

———. "The Women in Poe's Poems and Tales," *UTSE*, V (1925), 197–209.

Stroupe, John H. "Poe's Imaginary Voyage: Pym as Hero," *SSF*, IV, 315–21.

Swanson, Donald. "Poe's 'The Conqueror Worm,' " *Expl*, XIX (1961), Item 52.

Taft, Kendall. "The Identity of Poe's Martin Van Buren Mavis," *AL*, XXVI (1955), 562–63.

Tanasoca, Donald. "A Twentieth Century 'Stylus,' " *Sec News Sheet*, Bibliog Soc of the Univ of Va, No. 29, 1–2.

Tannenbaum, Earl. "Poe's Nicean Barks: 'Small Latin and Less Greek,' " *N & Q*, V (1958), 353–55.

Tanselle, G. T. "Poe and Vandenhoff Once More," *Am N & Q*, I, 101–102.

———. "An Unknown Early Appearance of 'The Raven,' " *SB*, XVI (1963), 220–23.

———. "Unrecorded Early Reprintings of Two Poe Tales" ("The Purloined Letter" and "The Oval Portrait"), *PBSA*, LVI, 252.

Tate, Allen. "The Angelic Imagination: Poe and the Power of Words," *KR*, XIV (1952), 455–75.

———. "Our Cousin, Mr. Poe," *PR* XVI (1949), 1207–19.

———. "Three Commentaries: Poe, James, and Joyce," *SR*, LVIII (1950), 1–15.

Taylor, Archer. "Poe's Dr. Lardner and 'Three Sundays in a Week,' " *Am N & Q*, III (1944), 153–55.

Taylor, Walter F. "Israfel in Motley," *SR*, XLII (1934), 330–39.

Thorner, H. E. "Hawthorne, Poe, and a Literary Ghost," *NEQ*, VII (1934), 146–54.

# Bibliography

Thorp, Willard. "Two Poe Letters at Princeton," *PULC*, X, 91–94.

Tinker, C. B. "Poetry and the Secret Impulse," *YR*, XVI (1927), 275–86.

Todd, William B. "The Early Issues of Poe's *Tales* (1845)," *LCUT*, VII, i, 13–18.

Townsend-Warner, Sylvia. "Cross Out Louisa," *New Statesman and Nation*, VIII (1934), 730.

Triplett, Edna B. "A Note on Poe's 'The Raven,' " *AL*, X (1938), 339–41.

Turner, Arlin. "Another Source of Poe's 'Julius Rodman,' " *AL*, VIII (1936), 69–70.

———. "A Note on Poe's 'Julius Rodman,' " *UTSE*, X (1930), 147–57.

———. "Sources of Poe's 'A Descent into the Maelstrom,' " *JEGP*, XLVI (1947), 298–301.

———, and T. O. Mabbott. "Two Poe Hoaxes By the Same Hand," *Am N & Q*, II (1943), 147–48.

"Unpublished Letter from Edgar Allan Poe, An," *Univ Mich Quarto*, No. 19.

Valéry, Paul. "Situation de Baudelaire," *Varieté*, II (1930), 141–47.

Valldeperes, Manuel. "El principio de trascendencia en la poesía de Edgar A. Poe," *Torre*, XIII (1965), 43–55.

Van Doorn, William. "Edgar Poe's 'Ulalume,' " *RLV*, XXIV (1958), 395–404.

Varnado, Seaborn. "The Numinous in the Work of Edgar Allan Poe," *DA*, XXVI, 3964–65.

Varner, Cornelia. "Notes on Poe's Use of Contemporary Materials in Certain of the Stories," *JEGP*, XXXII (1933), 77–80.

Varner, John G. "Note on a Poem Attributed to Poe"

("Impromptu: To Kate Carol"), *AL*, VIII (1936), 66–68.

———. "Poe and Miss Barrett of Wimpole Street," *Four Arts* (Richmond Va), II (Jan–Feb, 1935), 4–5.

———. "Poe's 'Tale of Jerusalem' and *The Talmud*," *ABC*, VI (1935), 56–57.

Vierra, Clifford. "Poe's 'Oblong Box': Factual Origins," *MLN*, LXXIV (1959), 693–95.

Vincent, H. P. "A Sarah Helen Whitman Letter about Edgar Allan Poe," *AL*, XIII (1941), 162–67.

Virtanen, Reino. "The Irradiations of *Eureka*: Valéry's Reflections on Poe's Cosmology," *TSLL*, VII (1962), 17–25.

Wainstein, Lia. "La situazione limite di E. A. Poe," *SA*, VI (1960), 73–86.

Walcutt, Charles C. "The Logic of Poe," *CE*, II (1941), 438–44.

Waldron, John. "Un classico del te rore spirituale" ("The Cask of Amontillado"), *FLe*, July 8, 1951, 7.

Walker, I. M. "The 'Legitimate Sources' of Terror in 'The Fall of the House of Usher,'" *MLR*, LXI (1966), 585–92.

Walker, Warren. "Poe's 'To Helen,'" *MLN*, LXXII (1957), 491–92.

Warfel, Harry R. "The Mathematics of Poe's Poetry," *CEA*, XXI (1959), v, 1, 5–6.

———. "Poe's Dr. Percival: A Note on 'The Fall of the House of Usher,'" *MLN*, LIV (1939), 129–31.

Wasserstrom, William. "The Spirit of Myrrha," *AL*, XIII (1956), 455–72.

Waterman, Arthur E. "Point of View in Poe" ("The Cask of Amontillado"), *CEA*, XXVII (1965), 5.

Watts, Charles. "Poe, Irving, and the *Southern Literary Messenger*," AL, XXVII (1955), 249–51.

———. "Washington Irving and Edgar Allan Poe," *Books at Brown*, XVIII (May, 1956), 10–13.

Webb, Howard. "Contributions to Poe's 'Penn Magazine,' " N & Q, V (1958), 447–48.

Weber, Jean-Paul. "Edgar Poe ou le thème de l'horloge," *NNRF*, Aug–Sept, 1958, 301–11, 498–508.

Wegelin, Oscar. "Poe's First Printer," *Am Col*, III (Oct, 1926), 31.

———. "The Printer of Poe's *Tamerlane*," NYHSQB, XXIV (1940), 23–25.

Weiss, Miriam. "Poe's Catterina," *MissQ*, XIX (1965), 29–33.

Weissbuch, T. N. "Edgar Allan Poe, Hoaxer in the American Tradition," NYHSQ, XLV (1961), 291–309.

Werner, W. L. "Poe's 'Israfel,' " *Expl*, II (1944), Item 44.

———. "Poe's Theories and Practice in Poetic Technique," AL, II (1930), 157–65.

West, Muriel. "Poe's 'Ligeia,' " *Expl*, XXII (1963), Item 15.

———. "Poe's 'Ligeia' and Isaac D'Israeli," CL, XVI (1964), 19–28.

Wetherill, P. M. "Edgar Allan Poe and Madame Sabatier," MLQ, XX (1959), 344–54.

Wetzel, George. "The Source of Poe's 'The Man That Was Used Up,' " N & Q, CXCVIII (1953), 38.

Whipple, William. "Poe, Clark, and 'Thingum Bob,' " AL, XXIX (1957), 312–16.

———. "Poe's Political Satire," *UTSE*, XXXV (1956), 81–95.

———. "Poe's Two-edged Satiric Tale," NCF, IX (1954), 121–33.

White, William. "Edgar Allan Poe: Magazine Journalist," *JQ*, XXXVIII (1961), 196–202.

Whiteside, M. B. "Poe and Dickinson," *Person*, XV (1934), 315–26.

Whitt, Celia. "Poe and *The Mysteries of Udolpho*," *UTSE*, XVII (1937), 124–31.

Whitty, J. H. "First and Last Publication of Poe's 'Raven,'" *Pub Weekly*, CXXX (Oct 17, 1936), 1635.

———. "A Parrot," *Colophon*, I (1935), 188–90.

———. "Poe's Writing Influenced by Richmond Gardens," *Richmond News Letter*, Apr 24, 1937.

Wiener, Philip P. "Poe's Logic and Metaphysic," *Person*, XIV (1933), 267–74.

Wilkinson, Ronald. "Poe's 'Balloon-Hoax' Once More," *AL*, XXXII (1960), 313–17.

———. "Poe's 'Hans Pfaall' Reconsidered," *N & Q*, XIII (1966), 333–37.

Williams, S. T. "New Letters about Poe," *YR*, XIV (1925), 755–73.

Williams, Valentine, and Alice Crawford. "The Detective in Fiction," *Fortnightly*, LXXVIII (1930), 380–92.

Wilson, Edmund. "Poe as a Literary Critic," *Nation*, CLV (Oct, 1942), 452–53.

———. "Poe at Home and Abroad," *New Republic*, XLIX (Dec 8, 1926), 77–80.

Wilson, James S. "The Devil Was In It," *Am Mer*, XIV (Oct, 1931), 215–20.

———. "The Personality of Poe," *VMHB*, LXVII (1959), 131–42.

———. "Poe's Philosophy of Composition," *No Am Rev*, 223 (Dec, 1926; Jan, Feb, 1927), 675–84.

———. "The Young Man Poe," *VQR*, II (1926), 238–53.

Wilt, Napier. "Poe's Attitude Toward His Tales: A New Document," *MP*, XXV (1927), 101–105.

Wimsatt, W. K., Jr. "A Further Note on Poe's 'Balloon Hoax,'" *AL*, XXII (1951), 491–92.

———. "Mary Rogers, John Anderson, and Others," *AL*, XXI (1950), 482–84.

———. "Poe and the Chess Automaton," *AL*, XI (1939), 138–51.

———. "Poe and the Mystery of Mary Rogers," *PMLA*, LV (1941), 230–48.

———. "What Poe Knew about Cryptography," *PMLA*, LVIII (1943), 754–79.

Winters, Yvor. "Edgar Allan Poe: A Crisis in the History of American Obscurantism," *AL*, VIII (1937), 379–401.

Wittlin, Joseph. "Poe in the Bronx," *PolR*, IV (1959), 3–14.

Worthen, Samuel C. "Poe and the Beautiful Cigar Girl," *AL*, XX (1948), 305–12.

———. "A Strange Aftermath of the Mystery of 'Marie Roget' (Mary Rogers)," *Proc NJ Hist Soc*, LX (1942), 116–23.

Wroth, L. C. "Poe's Baltimore," *Johns Hopkins Alumni Mag*, XVII (1929), 299–312.

Wuletich, Sybil. "Poe: The Rationale of the Uncanny," *DA*, XXII, 3675–76.

Wyld, Lionel. "The Enigma of Poe: Reality vs. L'Art pour L'Art," *LHB*, Ser 1, No. 2 (1960), 34–38.

Wylie, C. P. "Mathematical Allusions in Poe," *Sci Mo*, LXIII (1946), 227–35.

Young, Phillip. "The Early Psychologists and Poe," *AL*, XXII (1951), 442–54.

# Index